Business Use of Your Home

(Including Use by Daycare Providers)

For use in preparing

2014 Returns

Contents

Future Developments

For the latest information about developments related to Publication 587, such as legislation enacted after it was published, go to _www.irs.gov/pub587_.

Reminders

Simplified method for business use of home deduction. The IRS provides a simplified method to figure your expenses for business use of your home. For more information, see _Using the Simplified Method_ under _Figuring the Deduction_, later.

Photographs of missing children. The Internal Revenue Service is a proud partner with the National Center for Missing and Exploited Children. Photographs of missing children selected by the Center may appear in this publication on pages that would otherwise be blank. You can help bring these children home by looking at the photographs and calling 1-800-THE-LOST (1-800-843-5678) if you recognize a child.

Introduction

The purpose of this publication is to provide information on figuring and claiming the deduction for business use of your home. The term "home" includes a house, apartment, condominium, mobile home, boat, or similar property which provides basic living accommodations. It also includes structures on the property, such as an unattached garage, studio, barn, or greenhouse. However, it does not include any part of your property used exclusively as a hotel, motel, inn, or similar establishment.

Qualifying for a Deduction gives the requirements for qualifying to deduct expenses for the business use of your home (including special rules for employees and special rules for storing inventory or product samples). For special rules that apply to daycare providers, see _Daycare Facility_.

After you determine that you qualify for the deduction, _Figuring the Deduction_ explains the expenses you can deduct using either your actual expenses or the simplified method. The simplified method is an alternative to calculating and substantiating actual expenses.

Where To Deduct explains where a self-employed person, employee, or partner will report the deduction.

This publication also includes information on the following.

- Selling a home that was used partly for business.

- Deducting expenses for furniture and equipment used in your business.

- Records you should keep.

Finally, this publication contains worksheets to help you figure the amount of your deduction if you use your home in your farming business and you are filing Schedule F (Form 1040), you use your home for work as an employee, or you are a partner and the use of your home resulted in unreimbursed ordinary and necessary expenses that you are required to pay under the partnership agreement. If you used your home for business and you are filing Schedule C (Form 1040), you will use either Form 8829 or the Simplified Method Worksheet in your Instructions for Schedule C.

The rules in this publication apply to individuals.

If you need information on deductions for renting out your property, see Publication 527, Residential Rental Property.

Comments and suggestions. We welcome your comments about this publication and your suggestions for future editions.

You can send us comments from _www.irs.gov/formspubs_. Click on "More Information" and then on "Give us feedback."

Or you can write to:

Internal Revenue Service
Tax Forms and Publications
1111 Constitution Ave. NW, IR-6526
Washington, DC 20224

We respond to many letters by telephone. Therefore, it would be helpful if you would include your daytime phone number, including the area code, in your correspondence.

Although we cannot respond individually to each comment received, we do appreciate your feedback and will consider your comments as we revise our tax products.

Ordering forms and publications. Visit _www.irs.gov/formspubs_ to download forms and publications. Otherwise, you can go to _www.irs.gov/orderforms_ to order forms or call 1-800-829-3676 to order current and prior-year forms and instructions. Your order should arrive within 10 business days.

Tax questions. If you have a tax question, check the information available on IRS.gov or call 1-800-829-1040. We cannot answer tax questions sent to the above address.

Useful Items

You may want to see:

Publications

- ❏ **523** Selling Your Home

- ❏ **551** Basis of Assets

- ❏ **583** Starting a Business and Keeping Records

- ❏ **946** How To Depreciate Property

Forms (and Instructions)

- ❏ **Schedule C (Form 1040)** Profit or Loss from Business

- ❏ **2106** Employee Business Expenses

- ❏ **2106-EZ** Unreimbursed Employee Business Expenses

- ❏ **4562** Depreciation and Amortization

- ❏ **8829** Expenses for Business Use of Your Home

See _How To Get Tax Help_, near the end of this publication for information about getting publications and forms.

Qualifying for a Deduction

Generally, you cannot deduct items related to your home, such as mortgage interest, real estate taxes, utilities, maintenance, rent, depreciation, or property insurance, as business expenses. However, you may be able to deduct expenses related to the business use of part of your home if you meet specific requirements. Even then, the deductible amount of these types of expenses may be limited. Use this section and Figure A, later, to decide if you can deduct expenses for the business use of your home.

To qualify to deduct expenses for business use of your home, you must use part of your home:

- Exclusively and regularly as your principal place of business (defined later),

- Exclusively and regularly as a place where you meet or deal with patients, clients, or customers in the normal course of your trade or business,

- In the case of a separate structure which is not attached to your home, in connection with your trade or business,

- On a regular basis for certain storage use (see Storage of inventory or product samples, later),

- For rental use (see Publication 527), or

- As a daycare facility (see Daycare Facility, later).

Additional tests for employee use. If you are an employee and you use a part of your home for business, you may qualify for a deduction for its business use. You must meet the tests discussed earlier plus:

- Your business use must be for the convenience of your employer, and

- You must not rent any part of your home to your employer and use the rented portion to perform services as an employee for that employer.

If the use of the home office is merely appropriate and helpful, you cannot deduct expenses for the business use of your home.

Exclusive Use

To qualify under the exclusive use test, you must use a specific area of your home only for your trade or business. The area used for business can be a room or other separately identifiable space. The space does not need to be marked off by a permanent partition.

You do not meet the requirements of the exclusive use test if you use the area in question both for business and for personal purposes.

Example. You are an attorney and use a den in your home to write legal briefs and prepare clients' tax returns. Your family also uses the den for recreation. The den is not used exclusively in your trade or business, so you cannot claim a deduction for the business use of the den.

Exceptions to Exclusive Use

You do not have to meet the exclusive use test if either of the following applies.

- You use part of your home for the storage of inventory or product samples (discussed next).

- You use part of your home as a daycare facility, discussed later under Daycare Facility.

Note. With the exception of these two uses, any portion of the home used for business purposes must meet the exclusive use test.

Storage of inventory or product samples. If you use part of your home for storage of inventory or product samples, you can deduct expenses for the business use of your home without meeting the exclusive use test. However, you must meet all the following tests.

- You sell products at wholesale or retail as your trade or business.

- You keep the inventory or product samples in your home for use in your trade or business.

- Your home is the only fixed location of your trade or business.

- You use the storage space on a regular basis.

- The space you use is a separately identifiable space suitable for storage.

Example. Your home is the only fixed location of your business of selling mechanics' tools at retail. You regularly use half of your basement for storage of inventory and product samples. You sometimes use the area for personal purposes. The expenses for the storage space are deductible even though you do not use this part of your basement exclusively for business.

Regular Use

To qualify under the regular use test, you must use a specific area of your home for business on a regular basis. Incidental or occasional business use is not regular use. You must consider all facts and circumstances in determining whether your use is on a regular basis.

Trade or Business Use

To qualify under the trade-or-business-use test, you must use part of your home in connection with a trade or business. If you use your home for a profit-seeking activity that is not a trade or business, you cannot take a deduction for its business use.

Example. You use part of your home exclusively and regularly to read financial periodicals and reports, clip bond coupons, and carry out similar activities related to your own investments. You do not make investments as a broker or dealer. So, your activities are not part of a trade or business and you cannot take a deduction for the business use of your home.

Principal Place of Business

You can have more than one business location, including your home, for a single trade or business. To qualify to deduct the expenses for the business use of your home under the principal place of business test, your home must be your principal place of business for that trade or business. To determine whether your home is your principal place of business, you must consider:

- The relative importance of the activities performed at each place where you conduct business, and

- The amount of time spent at each place where you conduct business.

Your home office will qualify as your principal place of business if you meet the following requirements.

- You use it exclusively and regularly for administrative or management activities of your trade or business.

- You have no other fixed location where you conduct substantial administrative or management activities of your trade or business.

If, after considering your business locations, your home cannot be identified as your principal place of business, you cannot deduct home office expenses. However, see the later discussions under *Place To Meet Patients, Clients, or Customers* and *Separate Structure* for other ways to qualify to deduct home office expenses.

Administrative or management activities. There are many activities that are administrative or managerial in nature. The following are a few examples.

- Billing customers, clients, or patients.

- Keeping books and records.

- Ordering supplies.

- Setting up appointments.

- Forwarding orders or writing reports.

Administrative or management activities performed at other locations. The following activities performed by you or others will not disqualify your home office from being your principal place of business.

- You have others conduct your administrative or management activities at locations other than your home. (For example, another company does your billing from its place of business.)

- You conduct administrative or management activities at places that are not fixed locations of your business, such as in a car or a hotel room.

- You occasionally conduct minimal administrative or management activities at a fixed location outside your home.

- You conduct substantial nonadministrative or nonmanagement business activities at a fixed location outside your home. (For example, you meet with or provide services to customers, clients, or patients at a fixed location of the business outside your home.)

- You have suitable space to conduct administrative or management activities outside your home, but choose to use your home office for those activities instead.

Example 1. John is a self-employed plumber. Most of John's time is spent at customers' homes and offices installing and repairing plumbing. He has a small office in his home that he uses exclusively and regularly for the administrative or management activities of his business, such as phoning customers, ordering supplies, and keeping his books.

John writes up estimates and records of work completed at his customers' premises. He does not conduct any substantial administrative or management activities at any fixed location other than his home office. John does not do his own billing. He uses a local bookkeeping service to bill his customers.

John's home office qualifies as his principal place of business for deducting expenses for its use. He uses the home office for the administrative or managerial activities of his plumbing business and he has no other fixed location where he conducts these administrative or managerial activities. His choice to have his billing done by another company does not disqualify his home office from being his principal place of business. He meets all the qualifications, including principal place of business, so he can deduct expenses (subject to certain limitations, explained later) for the business use of his home.

Example 2. Pamela is a self-employed sales representative for several different product lines. She has an office in her home that she uses exclusively and regularly to set up appointments and write up orders and other reports for the companies whose products she sells. She occasionally writes up orders and sets up appointments from her hotel room when she is away on business overnight.

Pamela's business is selling products to customers at various locations throughout her territory. To make these sales, she regularly visits customers to explain the available products and take orders.

Pamela's home office qualifies as her principal place of business for deducting expenses for its use. She conducts administrative or management activities there and she has no other fixed location where she conducts substantial administrative or management activities. The fact that she conducts some administrative or management activities in her hotel room (not a fixed location) does not disqualify her home office from being her principal place of business. She meets all the qualifications, including principal place of business, so she can deduct expenses (subject to certain limitations, explained later) for the business use of her home.

Example 3. Paul is a self-employed anesthesiologist. He spends the majority of his time administering anesthesia and postoperative care in three local hospitals. One of the hospitals provides him with a small shared office where he could conduct administrative or management activities.

Paul very rarely uses the office the hospital provides. He uses a room in his home that he has converted to an

Figure A. Can You Deduct Business Use of the Home Expenses? Do not use this chart if you use your home for the storage of inventory or product samples, or to operate a daycare facility. See *Exceptions to Exclusive Use,* earlier, and *Daycare Facility,* later.

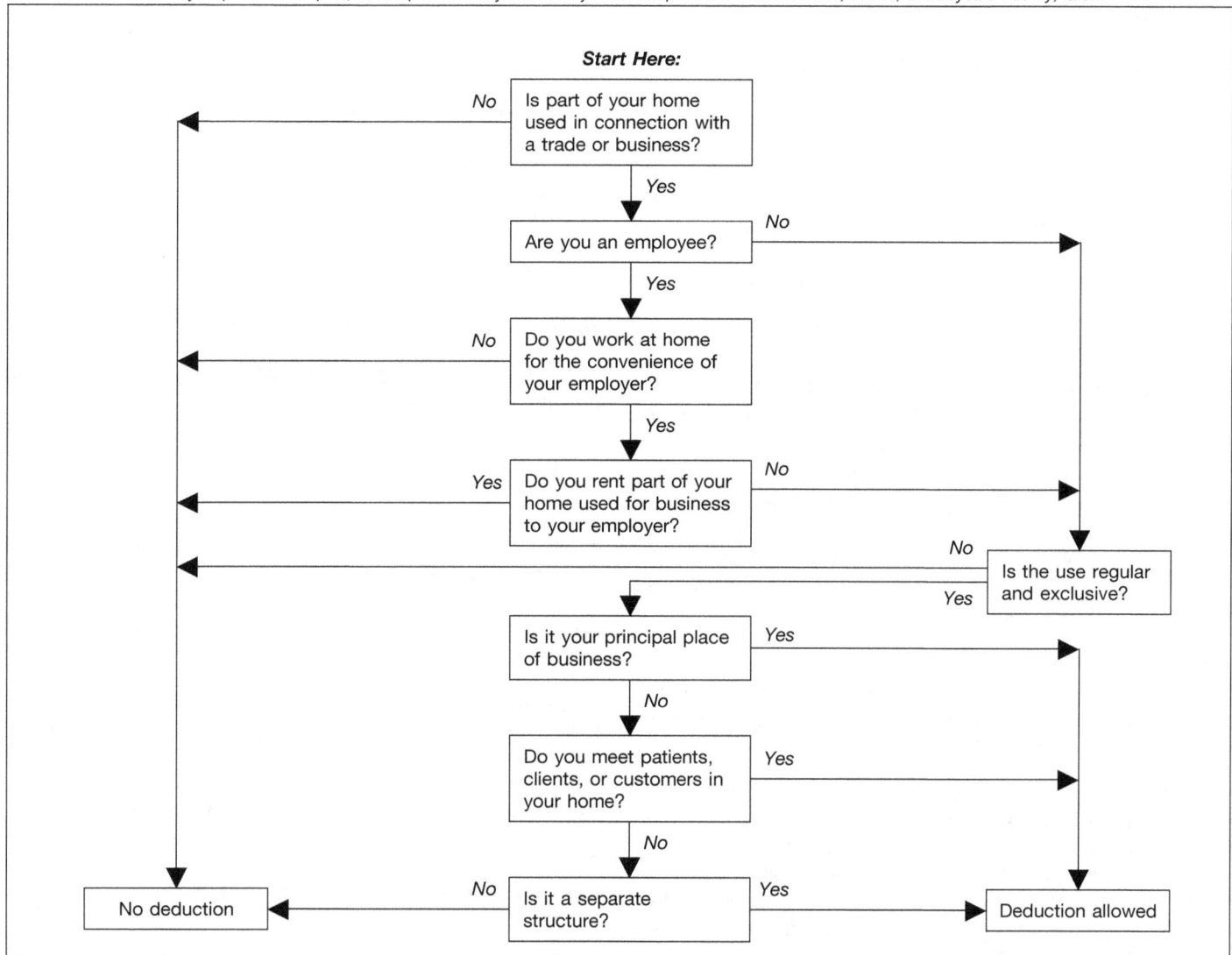

office. He uses this room exclusively and regularly to conduct all the following activities.

- Contacting patients, surgeons, and hospitals regarding scheduling.

- Preparing for treatments and presentations.

- Maintaining billing records and patient logs.

- Satisfying continuing medical education requirements.

- Reading medical journals and books.

Paul's home office qualifies as his principal place of business for deducting expenses for its use. He conducts administrative or management activities for his business as an anesthesiologist there and he has no other fixed location where he conducts substantial administrative or management activities for this business. His choice to use his home office instead of the one provided by the hospital does not disqualify his home office from being his principal place of business. His performance of substantial non-administrative or nonmanagement activities at fixed

locations outside his home also does not disqualify his home office from being his principal place of business. He meets all the qualifications, including principal place of business, so he can deduct expenses (subject to certain limitations, explained later) for the business use of his home.

Example 4. Kathleen is employed as a teacher. She is required to teach and meet with students at the school and to grade papers and tests. The school provides her with a small office where she can work on her lesson plans, grade papers and tests, and meet with parents and students. The school does not require her to work at home.

Kathleen prefers to use the office she has set up in her home and does not use the one provided by the school. She uses this home office exclusively and regularly for the administrative duties of her teaching job.

Kathleen must meet the convenience-of-the-employer test, even if her home qualifies as her principal place of business for deducting expenses for its use. Her employer provides her with an office and does not require her to work at home, so she does not meet the convenience-of-the-employer test and cannot claim a deduction for the business use of her home.

More Than One Trade or Business

The same home office can be the principal place of business for two or more separate business activities. Whether your home office is the principal place of business for more than one business activity must be determined separately for each of your trade or business activities. You must use the home office exclusively and regularly for one or more of the following purposes.

- As the principal place of business for one or more of your trades or businesses.

- As a place to meet or deal with patients, clients, or customers in the normal course of one or more of your trades or businesses.

- If your home office is a separate structure, in connection with one or more of your trades or businesses.

You can use your home office for more than one business activity, but you cannot use it for any nonbusiness (that is, personal) activities.

If you are an employee, any use of the home office in connection with your employment must be for the convenience of your employer. See _Rental to employer_, later, if you rent part of your home to your employer.

Example. Tracy White is employed as a teacher. Her principal place of work is the school, which provides her office space to do her school work. She also has a mail order jewelry business. All her work in the jewelry business is done in her home office and the office is used exclusively for that business. If she meets all the other tests, she can deduct expenses for the business use of her home for the jewelry business.

If Tracy also uses the office for work related to her teaching, she must meet the exclusive use test for both businesses to qualify for the deduction. As an employee, Tracy must also meet the convenience-of-the-employer test to qualify for the deduction. She does not meet this test for her work as a teacher, so she cannot claim a deduction for the business use of her home for either activity.

Place To Meet Patients, Clients, or Customers

If you meet or deal with patients, clients, or customers in your home in the normal course of your business, even though you also carry on business at another location, you can deduct your expenses for the part of your home used exclusively and regularly for business if you meet both the following tests.

- You physically meet with patients, clients, or customers on your premises.

- Their use of your home is substantial and integral to the conduct of your business.

Doctors, dentists, attorneys, and other professionals who maintain offices in their homes generally will meet this requirement.

Using your home for occasional meetings and telephone calls will not qualify you to deduct expenses for the business use of your home.

The part of your home you use exclusively and regularly to meet patients, clients, or customers does not have to be your principal place of business.

Example. June Quill, a self-employed attorney, works 3 days a week in her city office. She works 2 days a week in her home office used only for business. She regularly meets clients there. Her home office qualifies for a business deduction because she meets clients there in the normal course of her business.

Separate Structure

You can deduct expenses for a separate free-standing structure, such as a studio, workshop, garage, or barn, if you use it exclusively and regularly for your business. The structure does not have to be your principal place of business or a place where you meet patients, clients, or customers.

Example. John Berry operates a floral shop in town. He grows the plants for his shop in a greenhouse behind his home. He uses the greenhouse exclusively and regularly in his business, so he can deduct the expenses for its use, subject to certain limitations, explained later.

Figuring the Deduction

After you determine that you meet the tests under _Qualifying for a Deduction_, you can begin to figure how much you can deduct. When figuring the amount you can deduct for the business use of your home, you will use either your actual expenses or a simplified method.

Electing to use the simplified method. The simplified method is an alternative to the calculation, allocation, and substantiation of actual expenses. You choose whether or not to figure your deduction using the simplified method each tax year. See _Using the Simplified Method_, later.

Rental to employer. If you rent part of your home to your employer and you use the rented part in performing services for your employer as an employee, your deduction for the business use of your home is limited. You can deduct mortgage interest, qualified mortgage insurance premiums, real estate taxes, and personal casualty losses for the rented part, subject to any limitations. However, you cannot deduct otherwise allowable trade or business expenses, business casualty losses, or depreciation related to the use of your home (or use the simplified method as an alternative to deducting these actual expenses) in performing services for your employer.

Using Actual Expenses

If you do not or cannot elect to use the simplified method for a home, you will figure your deduction for that home using your actual expenses. You will also need to figure the percentage of your home used for business and the limit on the deduction.

If you are an employee or a partner, or you use your home in your farming business and you file Schedule F (Form 1040), you can use the Worksheet To Figure the Deduction for Business Use of Your Home, near the end of this publication, to help you figure your deduction. If you use your home in a trade or business and you file Schedule C (Form 1040), you will use Form 8829 to figure your deduction.

Part-year use. You cannot deduct expenses for the business use of your home incurred during any part of the year you did not use your home for business purposes. For example, if you begin using part of your home for business on July 1, and you meet all the tests from that date until the end of the year, consider only your expenses for the last half of the year in figuring your allowable deduction.

Expenses related to tax-exempt income. Generally, you cannot deduct expenses that are related to tax-exempt allowances. However, if you receive a tax-exempt parsonage allowance or a tax-exempt military allowance, your expenses for mortgage interest and real estate taxes are deductible under the normal rules. No deduction is allowed for other expenses related to the tax-exempt allowance.

If your housing is provided free of charge and the value of the housing is tax exempt, you cannot deduct the rental value of any portion of the housing.

Actual Expenses

You must divide the expenses of operating your home between personal and business use. The part of a home operating expense you can use to figure your deduction depends on both of the following.

- Whether the expense is direct, indirect, or unrelated.

- The percentage of your home used for business.

Table 1, next, describes the types of expenses you may have and the extent to which they are deductible.

Table 1. **Types of Expenses**

Expense	Description	Deductibility
Direct	Expenses only for the business part of your home.	Deductible in full.*
	Examples: Painting or repairs only in the area used for business.	Exception: May be only partially deductible in a daycare facility. See *Daycare Facility*, later.
Indirect	Expenses for keeping up and running your entire home.	Deductible based on the percentage of your home used for business.*
	Examples: Insurance, utilities, and general repairs.	
Unrelated	Expenses only for the parts of your home not used for business.	Not deductible.
	Examples: Lawn care or painting a room not used for business.	

*Subject to the deduction limit, discussed later.

 Form 8829 and the Worksheet To Figure the Deduction for Business Use of Your Home have separate columns for direct and indirect expenses.

Certain expenses are deductible whether or not you use your home for business. If you qualify to deduct business use of the home expenses, use the business percentage of these expenses to figure your total business use of the home deduction. These expenses include the following.

- Real estate taxes.

- Qualified mortgage insurance premiums.

- Deductible mortgage interest.

- Casualty losses.

Other expenses are deductible only if you use your home for business. You can use the business percentage of these expenses to figure your total business use of the home deduction. These expenses generally include (but are not limited to) the following.

- Depreciation (covered under *Depreciating Your Home*, later).

- Insurance.

- Rent paid for the use of property you do not own but use in your trade or business.

- Repairs.

- Security system.

- Utilities and services.

Real estate taxes. To figure the business part of your real estate taxes, multiply the real estate taxes paid by the percentage of your home used for business.

For more information on the deduction for real estate taxes, see Publication 530, Tax Information for Homeowners.

Deductible mortgage interest. To figure the business part of your deductible mortgage interest, multiply this interest by the percentage of your home used for business. You can include interest on a second mortgage in this computation. If your total mortgage debt is more than $1,000,000 or your home equity debt is more than $100,000, your deduction may be limited. For more information on what interest is deductible, see Publication 936, Home Mortgage Interest Deduction.

Qualified mortgage insurance premiums. To figure the business part of your qualified mortgage insurance premiums, multiply the premiums by the percentage of your home used for business. You can include premiums for insurance on a second mortgage in this computation. If your adjusted gross income is more than $100,000 ($50,000 if your filing status is married filing separately), your deduction may be limited. For more information, see Publication 936, and *Line 13* in the Instructions for Schedule A (Form 1040).

Casualty losses. If you have a casualty loss on your home that you use for business, treat the casualty loss as a direct expense, an indirect expense, or an unrelated expense, depending on the property affected.

- A direct expense is the loss on the portion of the property you use only in your business. Use the entire loss to figure the business use of the home deduction.

- An indirect expense is the loss on property you use for both business and personal purposes. Use only the business portion to figure the deduction.

- An unrelated expense is the loss on property you do not use in your business. Do not use any of the loss to figure the deduction.

Example. You meet the rules to take a deduction for an office in your home that is 10% of the total area of your house. A storm damages your roof. This is an indirect expense as the roof is part of the whole house and is considered to be used both for business and personal purposes. You would complete Form 4684, Casualties and Thefts, to report your loss. You complete both section A (Personal Use Property) and section B (Business and Income-Producing Property) as your home is used both for business and personal purposes. Since you use 90% of your home for personal purposes, use 90% of the cost or adjusted basis of your home, insurance or other reimbursement, and fair market value, both before and after the storm, to figure the amounts to enter on lines 2, 3, 5, and 6 of Form 4684. Since you use 10% of your home for business purposes, use 10% of the cost or adjusted basis of your home, insurance or other reimbursement, and fair market

value, both before and after the storm, to figure the amounts to enter on lines 20, 21, 23, and 24 of Form 4684.

Forms and worksheets to use. If you are filing Schedule C (Form 1040), get Form 8829 and follow the instructions for casualty losses. If you are an employee or a partner, or you file Schedule F (Form 1040), use the Worksheet To Figure the Deduction for Business Use of Your Home, near the end of this publication. You will also need Form 4684.

More information. For more information on casualty losses, see Publication 547, Casualties, Disasters, and Thefts.

Insurance. You can deduct the cost of insurance that covers the business part of your home. However, if your insurance premium gives you coverage for a period that extends past the end of your tax year, you can deduct only the business percentage of the part of the premium that gives you coverage for your tax year. You can deduct the business percentage of the part that applies to the following year in that year.

Rent. If you rent the home you occupy and meet the requirements for business use of the home, you can deduct part of the rent you pay. To figure your deduction, multiply your rent payments by the percentage of your home used for business.

If you own your home, you cannot deduct the fair rental value of your home. However, see *Depreciating Your Home*, later.

Repairs. The cost of repairs that relate to your business, including labor (other than your own labor), is a deductible expense. For example, a furnace repair benefits the entire home. If you use 10% of your home for business, you can deduct 10% of the cost of the furnace repair.

Repairs keep your home in good working order over its useful life. Examples of common repairs are patching walls and floors, painting, wallpapering, repairing roofs and gutters, and mending leaks. However, repairs are sometimes treated as a permanent improvement and are not deductible. See *Permanent improvements*, later, under *Depreciating Your Home*.

Security system. If you install a security system that protects all the doors and windows in your home, you can deduct the business part of the expenses you incur to maintain and monitor the system. You also can take a depreciation deduction for the part of the cost of the security system relating to the business use of your home.

Utilities and services. Expenses for utilities and services, such as electricity, gas, trash removal, and cleaning services, are primarily personal expenses. However, if you use part of your home for business, you can deduct the business part of these expenses. Generally, the business percentage for utilities is the same as the percentage of your home used for business.

Telephone. The basic local telephone service charge, including taxes, for the first telephone landline into your home is a nondeductible personal expense. However, charges for business long-distance phone calls on that line, as well as the cost of a second line into your home used exclusively for business, are deductible business expenses. Do not include these expenses as a cost of using your home for business. Deduct these charges separately on the appropriate form or schedule. For example, if you file Schedule C (Form 1040), deduct these expenses on line 25, Utilities (instead of line 30, Expenses for business use of your home).

Depreciating Your Home

If you own your home and qualify to deduct expenses for its business use, you can claim a deduction for depreciation. Depreciation is an allowance for the wear and tear on the part of your home used for business. You cannot depreciate the cost or value of the land. You recover its cost when you sell or otherwise dispose of the property.

Before you figure your depreciation deduction, you need to know the following information.

- The month and year you started using your home for business.

- The adjusted basis and fair market value of your home (excluding land) at the time you began using it for business.

- The cost of any improvements before and after you began using the property for business.

- The percentage of your home used for business. See *Business Percentage*, later.

Adjusted basis defined. The adjusted basis of your home is generally its cost, plus the cost of any permanent improvements you made to it, minus any casualty losses or depreciation deducted in earlier tax years. For a discussion of adjusted basis, see Publication 551, Basis of Assets.

Permanent improvements. A permanent improvement increases the value of property, adds to its life, or gives it a new or different use. Examples of improvements are replacing electric wiring or plumbing, adding a new roof or addition, paneling, or remodeling.

You must carefully distinguish between repairs and improvements. See *Repairs*, earlier, under *Actual Expenses*. You also must keep accurate records of these expenses. These records will help you decide whether an expense is a deductible or a capital (added to the basis) expense. However, if you make repairs as part of an extensive remodeling or restoration of your home, the entire job is an improvement.

Example. You buy an older home and fix up two rooms as a beauty salon. You patch the plaster on the ceilings and walls, paint, repair the floor, install an outside door, and install new wiring, plumbing, and other equipment. Normally, the patching, painting, and floor work are repairs and the other expenses are permanent improvements. However, because the work gives your property a new use, the entire remodeling job is a permanent

improvement and its cost is added to the basis of the property. You cannot deduct any portion of it as a repair expense.

Adjusting for depreciation deducted in earlier years. Decrease the basis of your property by the depreciation you deducted, or could have deducted, on your tax returns under the method of depreciation you properly selected. If you deducted less depreciation than you could have under the method you selected, decrease the basis by the amount you could have deducted under that method. If you did not deduct any depreciation, decrease the basis by the amount you could have deducted.

If you deducted more depreciation than you should have, decrease your basis by the amount you should have deducted, plus the part of the excess depreciation you deducted that actually decreased your tax liability for any year.

If you deducted the incorrect amount of depreciation, see Publication 946, How To Depreciate Property.

Fair market value defined. The fair market value of your home is the price at which the property would change hands between a buyer and a seller, neither having to buy or sell, and both having reasonable knowledge of all necessary facts. Sales of similar property, on or about the date you begin using your home for business, may be helpful in determining the property's fair market value.

Figuring the depreciation deduction for the current year. If you began using your home for business before 2014, continue to use the same depreciation method you used in past tax years. However, if you figured your deduction for business use of the home using the simplified method in a prior year, you will need to use the optional depreciation table for modified accelerated cost recovery system (MACRS) property. See Publication 946 for the optional depreciation tables. For more information about the simplified method, see Revenue Procedure 2013-13, 2013-06 I.R.B. 478, available at *www.irs.gov/irb/2013-06_IRB/ar09.html*.

If you began using your home for business for the first time in 2014, depreciate the business part as nonresidential real property under MACRS. Under MACRS, nonresidential real property is depreciated using the straight line method over 39 years. For more information on MACRS and other methods of depreciation, see Publication 946.

To figure the depreciation deduction, you must first figure the part of the cost of your home that can be depreciated (depreciable basis). The depreciable basis is figured by multiplying the percentage of your home used for business by the smaller of the following.

- The adjusted basis of your home (excluding land) on the date you began using your home for business.

- The fair market value of your home (excluding land) on the date you began using your home for business.

Depreciation table. If 2014 was the first year you used your home for business, you can figure your 2014 depreciation for the business part of your home by using the appropriate percentage from the following table.

Table 2. MACRS Percentage Table for 39-Year Nonresidential Real Property

Month First Used for Business	Percentage To Use
1	2.461%
2	2.247%
3	2.033%
4	1.819%
5	1.605%
6	1.391%
7	1.177%
8	0.963%
9	0.749%
10	0.535%
11	0.321%
12	0.107%

Multiply the depreciable basis of the business part of your home by the percentage from the table for the first month you use your home for business. See Publication 946 for the percentages for the remaining tax years of the recovery period.

Example. In May, George Miller began to use one room in his home exclusively and regularly to meet clients. This room is 8% of the square footage of his home. He bought the home in 2004 for $125,000. He determined from his property tax records that his adjusted basis in the house (exclusive of land) is $115,000. In May, the house had a fair market value of $165,000. He multiplies his adjusted basis of $115,000 (which is less than the fair market value) by 8%. The result is $9,200, his depreciable basis for the business part of the house.

George files his return based on the calendar year. May is the 5th month of his tax year. He multiplies his depreciable basis of $9,200 by 1.605% (.01605), the percentage from the table for the 5th month. His depreciation deduction is $147.66.

Depreciating permanent improvements. Add the costs of permanent improvements made before you began using your home for business to the basis of your property. Depreciate these costs as part of the cost of your home as explained earlier. The costs of improvements made after you begin using your home for business (that affect the business part of your home, such as a new roof) are depreciated separately. Multiply the cost of the improvement by the business-use percentage and depreciate the result over the recovery period that would apply to your home if you began using it for business at the same time as the improvement. For improvements made this year, the recovery period is 39 years. For the percentage to use for the first year, see Table 2, earlier. For more information on recovery periods, see Publication 946.

Business Percentage

To find the business percentage, compare the size of the part of your home that you use for business to your whole house. Use the resulting percentage to figure the business part of the expenses for operating your entire home.

You can use any reasonable method to determine the business percentage. The following are two commonly used methods for figuring the percentage.

1. Divide the area (length multiplied by the width) used for business by the total area of your home.

2. If the rooms in your home are all about the same size, you can divide the number of rooms used for business by the total number of rooms in your home.

Example 1.

- Your office is 240 square feet (12 feet × 20 feet).

- Your home is 1,200 square feet.

- Your office is 20% (240 ÷ 1,200) of the total area of your home.

- Your business percentage is 20%.

Example 2.

- You use one room in your home for business.

- Your home has 10 rooms, all about equal size.

- Your office is 10% (1 ÷ 10) of the total area of your home.

- Your business percentage is 10%.

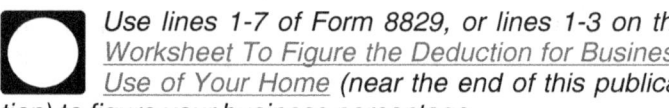 *Use lines 1-7 of Form 8829, or lines 1-3 on the Worksheet To Figure the Deduction for Business Use of Your Home (near the end of this publication) to figure your business percentage.*

Deduction Limit

If your gross income from the business use of your home equals or exceeds your total business expenses (including depreciation), you can deduct all your business expenses related to the use of your home.

If your gross income from the business use of your home is less than your total business expenses, your deduction for certain expenses for the business use of your home is limited.

Your deduction of otherwise nondeductible expenses, such as insurance, utilities, and depreciation of your home (with depreciation of your home taken last), that are allocable to the business, is limited to the gross income from the business use of your home minus the sum of the following.

1. The business part of expenses you could deduct even if you did not use your home for business (such as mortgage interest, real estate taxes, and casualty and

theft losses that are allowable as itemized deductions on Schedule A (Form 1040)). These expenses are discussed in detail under *Actual Expenses*, earlier.

2. The business expenses that relate to the business activity in the home (for example, business phone, supplies, and depreciation on equipment), but not to the use of the home itself.

If you are self-employed, do not include in (2) above your deduction for one-half of your self-employment tax.

Carryover of unallowed expenses. If your deductions are greater than the current year's limit, you can carry over the excess to the next year in which you use actual expenses. They are subject to the deduction limit for that year, whether or not you live in the same home during that year.

Figuring the deduction limit and carryover. If you are an employee or a partner, or you file Schedule F (Form 1040), use the Worksheet To Figure the Deduction for Business Use of Your Home, near the end of this publication. If you file Schedule C (Form 1040), figure your deduction limit and carryover on Form 8829.

Example. You meet the requirements for deducting expenses for the business use of your home. You use 20% of your home for business. In 2014, your business expenses and the expenses for the business use of your home are deducted from your gross income in the following order.

Gross income from business	$6,000
Minus:	
Deductible mortgage interest and real estate taxes (20%)	3,000
Business expenses not related to the use of your home (100%) (business phone, supplies, and depreciation on equipment)	2,000
Deduction limit	$1,000
Minus other expenses allocable to business use of home:	
Maintenance, insurance, and utilities (20%)	800
Depreciation allowed (20% = $1,600 allowable, but subject to balance of deduction limit)	200
Other expenses up to the deduction limit	$1,000
Depreciation carryover to 2015 ($1,600 – $200) (subject to deduction limit in 2015)	$1,400

You can deduct all of the business part of your deductible mortgage interest and real estate taxes ($3,000). You also can deduct all of your business expenses not related to the use of your home ($2,000). Additionally, you can deduct all of the business part of your expenses for maintenance, insurance, and utilities, because the total ($800) is less than the $1,000 deduction limit. Your deduction for depreciation for the business use of your home is limited to $200 ($1,000 minus $800) because of the deduction limit. You can carry over the $1,400 balance and add it to your depreciation for 2015, subject to your deduction limit in 2015.

More than one place of business. If part of the gross income from your trade or business is from the business use of part of your home and part is from a place other than your home, you must determine the part of your gross income from the business use of your home before you figure the deduction limit. In making this determination, consider the time you spend at each location, the business investment in each location, and any other relevant facts and circumstances.

⬤ *If your home office qualifies as your principal place of business, you can deduct your daily transportation costs between your home and another work location in the same trade or business. For more information on transportation costs, see Publication 463, Travel, Entertainment, Gift, and Car Expenses.*

Using the Simplified Method

The simplified method is an alternative to the calculation, allocation, and substantiation of actual expenses. In most cases, you will figure your deduction by multiplying $5, the prescribed rate, by the area of your home used for a qualified business use. The area you use to figure your deduction is limited to 300 square feet. See *Simplified Amount*, later, for information about figuring the amount of the deduction.

For more information about the simplified method, see Revenue Procedure 2013-13, 2013-06 I.R.B. 478, available at www.irs.gov/irb/2013-06_IRB/ar09.html.

Actual expenses and depreciation of your home. If you elect to use the simplified method, you cannot deduct any actual expenses for the business except for business expenses that are not related to the use of the home. You also cannot deduct any depreciation (including any additional first-year depreciation) or section 179 expense for the portion of the home that is used for a qualified business use. The depreciation deduction allowable for that portion of the home is deemed to be zero for a year you use the simplified method. If you figure your deduction for business use of the home using actual expenses in a subsequent year, you will have to use the appropriate optional depreciation table for MACRS to figure your depreciation.

More information. For more information about claiming depreciation in a subsequent year, see Revenue Procedure 2013-13, 2013-06 I.R.B. 478, available at www.irs.gov/irb/2013-06_IRB/ar09.html. See Publication 946 for the optional depreciation tables.

⬤ *Although you cannot deduct any depreciation or section 179 expense for the portion of your home used for a qualified business use, you may still claim depreciation or the section 179 expense deduction on other assets used in the business (for example, furniture and equipment).*

Expenses deductible without regard to business use. When using the simplified method, treat as personal expenses those business expenses related to the use of the home that are deductible without regard to whether there is a qualified business use of the home. These expenses include mortgage interest, real estate taxes, and casualty losses, subject to any limitations. See *Where To Deduct*, later. If you also rent part of your home, you must still allocate these expenses between rental use and personal use (for this purpose, personal use includes business use reported using the simplified method).

No deduction of carryover of actual expenses. If you used actual expenses to figure your deduction for business use of the home in a prior year and your deduction was limited, you cannot deduct the disallowed amount carried over from the prior year during a year you figure your deduction using the simplified method. Instead, you will continue to carry over the disallowed amount to the next year that you use actual expenses to figure your deduction.

Electing the Simplified Method

You choose whether or not to figure your deduction using the simplified method each tax year. Make the election for a home by using the simplified method to figure the deduction for the qualified business use of that home on a timely filed, original federal income tax return. An election for a tax year, once made, is irrevocable. A change from using the simplified method in one year to actual expenses in a succeeding tax year, or *vice-versa*, is not a change in method of accounting and does not require the consent of the Commissioner.

Shared use. If you share your home with someone else who also uses the home in a business that qualifies for this deduction, each of you make your own election.

More than one qualified business use. If you conduct more than one business that qualifies for this deduction in your home, your election to use the simplified method applies to all your qualified business uses of that home.

More than one home. If you used more than one home in your business during the year (for example, you moved during the year), you can elect to use the simplified method for only one of the homes. You must figure the deduction for any other home using actual expenses.

Simplified Amount

Your deduction for the qualified business use of a home is the sum of each amount you figure for a separate qualified business use of your home. To figure your deduction for the business use of a home using the simplified method, you will need to know the following information for each qualified business use of the home.

- The allowable area of your home used in conducting the business. If you did not conduct the business for the entire year in the home or the area changed during the year, you will need to know the allowable area you used and the number of days you conducted the business for each month.

- The gross income from the business use of your home.

- The amount of the business expenses that are not related to the use of your home.

- If the qualified business use is for a daycare facility that uses space in your home on a regular (but not exclusive) basis, you will also need to know the percentage of time that part of your home is used for daycare.

To figure the amount you can deduct for qualified business use of your home using the simplified method, follow these 3 steps.

1. Multiply the allowable area by $5 (or less than $5 if the qualified business use is for a daycare that uses space in your home on a regular, but not exclusive, basis). See *Allowable area* and *Space used regularly for daycare*, later.

2. Subtract the expenses from the business that are not related to the use of the home from the gross income related to the business use of the home. If these expenses are greater than the gross income from the business use of the home, then you cannot take a deduction for this business use of the home. See *Gross income limitation*, later.

3. Take the smaller of the amounts from (1) and (2). This is the amount you can deduct for this qualified business use of your home using the simplified method.

If you are an employee or a partner, or you use your home in your farming business and file Schedule F (Form 1040), you can use the Simplified Method Worksheet, near the end of this publication, to help you figure your deduction. If you use your home in a trade or business and you file Schedule C (Form 1040), you will use the Simplified Method Worksheet in your Instructions for Schedule C to figure your deduction.

Allowable area. In most cases, the allowable area is the smaller of the actual area (in square feet) of your home used in conducting the business and 300 square feet. Your allowable area may be smaller if you conducted the business as a qualified joint venture with your spouse, the area used by the business was shared with another qualified business use, you used the home for the business for only part of the year, or the area used by the business changed during the year. You can use the Area Adjustment Worksheet (for simplified method), near the end of this publication, to help you figure your allowable area for a qualified business use.

Area used by a qualified joint venture. If the qualified business use of the home is also a qualified joint venture, you and your spouse will figure the deduction for the business use separately. Split the actual area used in conducting business between you and your spouse in the same manner you split your other tax attributes. Then, each spouse will figure the allowable area separately. For more information about qualified joint ventures, see *Qualified Joint Venture* in the Instructions for Schedule C.

Shared use. If you share your home with someone else who uses the home to conduct business that also qualifies for this deduction, you may not include the same square feet to figure your deduction as the other person.

You must allocate the shared space between you and the other person in a reasonable manner.

Example. Kristen and Lindsey are roommates. Kristen uses 300 square feet of their home for a qualified business use. Lindsey uses 200 square feet of their home for a separate qualified business use. The qualified business uses share 100 square feet. In addition to the portion that they do not share, Kristen and Lindsey can both claim 50 of the 100 square feet or divide the 100 square feet between them in any reasonable manner. If divided evenly, Kristen could claim 250 square feet using the simplified method and Lindsey could claim 150 square feet.

More than one qualified business use. If you conduct more than one business qualifying for the deduction, you are limited to a maximum of 300 square feet for all of the businesses. Allocate the actual square footage used (up to the maximum of 300 square feet) among your qualified business uses in a reasonable manner. However, do not allocate more square feet to a qualified business use than you actually use for that business.

Rental use. The simplified method does not apply to rental use. A rental use that qualifies for the deduction must be figured using actual expenses. If the rental use and a qualified business use share the same area, you will have to allocate the actual area used between the two uses. You cannot use the same area to figure a deduction for the qualified business use as you are using to figure the deduction for the rental use.

Part-year use or area changes (for simplified method only). If your qualified business use was for a portion of the year (for example, a seasonal business, a business that begins during the year, or you moved during the year) or you changed the square footage of your qualified business use, your deduction is limited to the average monthly allowable square footage. You calculate the average monthly allowable square footage by adding the amount of allowable square feet you used in each month and dividing the sum by 12. When determining the average monthly allowable square footage, you cannot take more than 300 square feet into account for any one month. Additionally, if your qualified business use was less than 15 days in a month, you must use -0- for that month.

Example 1. Andy files his federal income tax return on a calendar year basis. On July 20, he began using 420 square feet of his home for a qualified business use. He continued to use the 420 square feet until the end of the year. His average monthly allowable square footage is 125 square feet, which is figured using 300 square feet for each month August through December divided by the number of months in the year ((0 + 0 + 0 + 0 + 0 + 0 + 0 + 300 + 300 + 300 + 300 + 300)/12).

Example 2. Amy files her federal income tax return on a calendar year basis. On April 20, she began using 100 square feet of her home for a qualified business use. On August 5, she expanded the area of her qualified use to 330 square feet. Amy continued to use the 330 square feet until the end of the year. Her average monthly allowable square footage is 150 square feet, which is figured using 100 square feet for May through July and 300 square feet for August through December divided by the number of months in the year ((0 + 0 + 0 + 0 + 100 + 100 +100 + 300 + 300 + 300 + 300 + 300)/12).

Example 3. Donna files her federal income tax return on a calendar year basis. From January 1 through July 16 she used 300 square feet of her home for a qualified business use. On July 17, Donna moved to a new home and immediately began using 200 square feet for the same qualified business use. While preparing her tax return, Donna decided to use the simplified method to deduct her qualified business use of the first home and files a Form 8829 to deduct her qualified business use of the second home. Her average monthly allowable square footage is 175 square feet, which is figured using 300 square feet for January through July divided by the number of months in the year ((300 +300 +300 + 300 + 300 + 300 + 300 + 0 + 0 + 0 + 0 + 0)/12).

 If you moved during the year, your average allowable square footage will generally be less than 300.

Gross income limitation. Your deduction for business use of the home is limited to an amount equal to the gross income derived from the qualified business use of the home reduced by the business deductions that are unrelated to the use of your home. If the business deductions that are unrelated to the use of your home are greater than the gross income derived from the qualified business use of your home, then you cannot take a deduction for this qualified business use of your home.

Business expenses not related to use of the home. These expenses relate to the business activity in the home, but not to the use of the home itself. You can still deduct business expenses that are unrelated to the use of the home. See *Where To Deduct*, later. Examples of business expenses that are unrelated to the use of the home are advertising, wages, supplies, dues, and depreciation for equipment.

Space used regularly for daycare. If you do not use the area of your home exclusively for daycare, you must reduce the prescribed rate (maximum $5 per square foot) before figuring your deduction. The reduced rate will equal the prescribed rate times a fraction. The numerator of the fraction is the number of hours that the space was used during the year for daycare and the denominator is the total number of hours during the year that the space was available for all uses. You can use the Daycare Facility Worksheet (for simplified method), near the end of this publication, to help you figure the reduced rate.

If you used at least 300 square feet for daycare regularly and exclusively during the year, then you do not need to reduce the prescribed rate or complete the Daycare Facility Worksheet.

Daycare Facility

If you use space in your home on a regular basis for providing daycare, you may be able to claim a deduction for that part of your home even if you use the same space for nonbusiness purposes. To qualify for this exception to the exclusive use rule, you must meet both of the following requirements.

- You must be in the trade or business of providing daycare for children, persons age 65 or older, or persons who are physically or mentally unable to care for themselves.

- You must have applied for, been granted, or be exempt from having, a license, certification, registration, or approval as a daycare center or as a family or group daycare home under state law. You do not meet this requirement if your application was rejected or your license or other authorization was revoked.

Figuring the deduction. If you elect to use the simplified method for your home, figure your deduction as described earlier in *Using the Simplified Method* under *Figuring the Deduction*.

If you are figuring your deduction using actual expenses and you regularly use part of your home for daycare, figure what part is used for daycare, as explained in *Business Percentage*, earlier, under *Figuring the Deduction*. If you also use that part exclusively for daycare, deduct all the allocable expenses, subject to the deduction limit, as explained earlier.

If the use of part of your home as a daycare facility is regular, but not exclusive, you must figure the percentage of time that part of your home is used for daycare. A room that is available for use throughout each business day and that you regularly use in your business is considered to be used for daycare throughout each business day. You do not have to keep records to show the specific hours the area was used for business. You can use the area occasionally for personal reasons. However, a room you use only occasionally for business does not qualify for the deduction.

⬤ *To find the percentage of time you actually use your home for business, compare the total time used for business to the total time that part of your home can be used for all purposes. You can compare the hours of business use in a week with the number of hours in a week (168). Or you can compare the hours of business use for the year with the number of hours in the year (8,760 in 2014). If you started or stopped using your home for daycare in 2014, you must prorate the number of hours based on the number of days the home was available for daycare.*

Example 1. Mary Lake used her basement to operate a daycare business for children. She figures the business percentage of the basement as follows.

$$\frac{\text{Square footage of the basement}}{\text{Square footage of her home}} = \frac{1,600}{3,200} = 50\%$$

She used the basement for daycare an average of 12 hours a day, 5 days a week, for 50 weeks a year. During the other 12 hours a day, the family could use the basement. She figures the percentage of time the basement was used for daycare as follows.

$$\frac{\text{Number of hours used for daycare (12 x 5 x 50)}}{\text{Total number of hours in the year (24 x 365)}} = \frac{3,000}{8,760} = 34.25\%$$

Mary can deduct 34.25% of any direct expenses for the basement. However, because her indirect expenses are for the entire house, she can deduct only 17.13% of the indirect expenses. She figures the percentage for her indirect expenses as follows.

Business percentage of the basement	50%
Multiplied by: Percentage of time used for daycare	× 34.25%
Percentage for indirect expenses	17.13%

Mary completes Form 8829, Part I, figuring the percentage of her home used for business, including the percentage of time the basement was used.

In Part II, Mary figures her deductible expenses. She uses the following information to complete Part II.

Gross income from her daycare business	$50,000
Expenses not related to the business use of the home . . .	$25,000
Tentative profit	$25,000
Rent	$8,400
Utilities	$850
Painting the basement	$500

Mary enters her tentative profit, $25,000, on line 8. (This figure is the same as the amount on line 29 of her Schedule C (Form 1040).)

The expenses she paid for rent and utilities relate to her entire home. Therefore, she enters the amount paid for rent on line 18, column (b), and the amount paid for utilities on line 20, column (b). She shows the total of these expenses on line 22, column (b). For line 23, she multiplies the amount on line 22, column (b) by the percentage on line 7 and enters the result, $1,585.

Mary paid $500 to have the basement painted. The painting is a direct expense. However, because she did not use the basement exclusively for daycare, she must multiply $500 by the percentage of time the basement was used for daycare (34.25% – line 6). She enters $171 (34.25% × $500) on line 19, column (a). She adds line 22, column (a), and line 23 and enters $1,756 ($171 + $1,585) on line 25. This is less than her deduction limit (line 15), so she can deduct the entire amount. She follows the instructions to complete the rest of Part II and enters $1,756 on lines 33 and 35. She then carries the $1,756 to line 30 of her Schedule C (Form 1040).

Example 2. Assume the same facts as in *Example 1* except that Mary also has another room that was available each business day for children to take naps in. Although she did not keep a record of the number of hours the room was actually used for naps, it was used for part of each business day. Since the room was available for business use during regular operating hours each business day and was used regularly in the business, it is considered used for daycare throughout each business day. The basement and room are 60% of the total area of her home. In figuring her expenses, 34.25% of any direct expenses for the basement and room are deductible. In addition, 20.55% (34.25% × 60%) of her indirect expenses are deductible.

Example 3. Assume the same facts as in *Example 1* except that Mary stopped using her home for a daycare facility on June 24, 2014. She used the basement for daycare an average of 12 hours a day, 5 days a week, but for only 25 weeks of the year. During the other 12 hours a day, the family could still use the basement. She figures the percentage of time the basement was used for business as follows.

$$\frac{\text{Number of hours used for daycare (12 x 5 x 25)}}{\text{Total number of hours during period used (24 x 175)}} = \frac{1,500}{4,200} = 35.71\%$$

Mary can deduct 35.71% of any direct expenses for the basement. However, because her indirect expenses are for the entire house, she can deduct only 17.86% of the indirect expenses. She figures the percentage for her indirect expenses as follows.

Business percentage of the basement	50%
Multiplied by: Percentage of time used for daycare	× 35.71%
Percentage for indirect expenses	17.86%

Meals. If you provide food for your daycare recipients, do not include the expense as a cost of using your home for business. Claim it as a separate deduction on your Schedule C (Form 1040). You can never deduct the cost of food consumed by you or your family. You can deduct as a business expense 100% of the actual cost of food consumed by your daycare recipients (see *Standard meal and snack rates*, later, for an optional method for eligible children) and generally only 50% of the cost of food consumed by your employees. However, you can deduct 100% of the cost of food consumed by your employees if its value can be excluded from their wages as a *de minimis* fringe benefit. For more information on meals that meet these requirements, see *Meals* in chapter 2 of Publication 15-B, Employer's Tax Guide to Fringe Benefits.

If you deduct the actual cost of food for your daycare business, keep a separate record (with receipts) of your family's food costs.

Reimbursements you receive from a sponsor under the Child and Adult Care Food Program of the Department of Agriculture are taxable only to the extent they exceed your expenses for food for eligible children. If your reimbursements are more than your expenses for food, show the difference as income in Part I of Schedule C (Form 1040). If your food expenses are greater than the reimbursements, show the difference as an expense in Part V of Schedule C (Form 1040). Do not include payments or expenses for your own children if they are eligible for the program. Follow this procedure even if you receive a Form 1099-MISC, Miscellaneous Income, reporting a payment from the sponsor.

Standard meal and snack rates. If you qualify as a family daycare provider, you can use the standard meal and snack rates, instead of actual costs, to compute the deductible cost of meals and snacks provided to eligible children. For these purposes:

- A family daycare provider is a person engaged in the business of providing family daycare.

- Family daycare is childcare provided to eligible children in the home of the family daycare provider. The care must be non-medical, not involve a transfer of legal custody, and generally last less than 24 hours each day.

- Eligible children are minor children receiving family daycare in the home of the family daycare provider. Eligible children do not include children who are full-time or part-time residents in the home where the childcare is provided or children whose parents or guardians are residents of the same home. Eligible children do not include children who receive daycare services for personal reasons of the provider. For example, if a provider provides daycare services for a relative as a favor to that relative, that child is not an eligible child.

You can compute the deductible cost of each meal and snack you actually purchased and served to an eligible child during the time period you provided family daycare using the standard meal and snack rates shown in Table 3, later. You can use the standard meal and snack rates for a maximum of one breakfast, one lunch, one dinner, and three snacks per eligible child per day. If you receive reimbursement for a particular meal or snack, you can deduct only the portion of the applicable standard meal or snack rate that is more than the amount of the reimbursement.

You can use either the standard meal and snack rates or actual costs to calculate the deductible cost of food provided to eligible children in the family daycare for any particular tax year. If you choose to use the standard meal and snack rates for a particular tax year, you must use the rates for all your deductible food costs for eligible children during that tax year. However, if you use the standard meal and snack rates in any tax year, you can use actual costs to compute the deductible cost of food in any other tax year.

If you use the standard meal and snack rates, you must maintain records to substantiate the computation of the total amount deducted for the cost of food provided to eligible children. The records kept should include the name of each child, dates and hours of attendance in the daycare, and the type and quantity of meals and snacks served. This information can be recorded in a log similar to the one shown in Exhibit A, near the end of this publication.

The standard meal and snack rates include beverages, but do not include non-food supplies used for food preparation, service, or storage, such as containers, paper products, or utensils. These expenses can be claimed as a separate deduction on your Schedule C (Form 1040).

Table 3. Standard Meal and Snack Rates[1]

Location of Family Daycare Provider	Breakfast	Lunch	Dinner	Snack
States other than Alaska and Hawaii	$1.28	$2.40	$2.40	$0.71
Alaska	$2.04	$3.89	$3.89	$1.16
Hawaii	$1.49	$2.81	$2.81	$0.83

[1] The applicable rates for 2014 are the Child and Adult Care Food Program reimbursement rates in effect on December 31, 2013.

Sale or Exchange of Your Home

If you sell or exchange your home, you may be able to exclude up to $250,000 ($500,000 for certain married persons filing a joint return) of the gain on the sale or exchange if you meet the ownership and use tests.

Ownership and use tests. To qualify for the exclusion, you must meet the ownership and use tests. This means that during the 5-year period ending on the date of the sale:

- You owned the home for at least 2 years (ownership test), and
- You lived in the home as your main home for at least 2 years (use test).

Gain on Sale

If you use property partly as a home and partly for business, the treatment of any gain on the sale varies depending on whether the part of the property used for business is part of your home or separate from it.

Part of Home Used for Business

If the part of your property used for business is within your home, such as a room used as a home office for a business or rooms used to provide daycare, you do not need to allocate gain on the sale of the property between the business part of the property and the part used as a home. In addition, you do not need to report the sale of the business part on Form 4797, Sales of Business Property. This is true whether or not you were entitled to claim any depreciation. However, you cannot exclude the part of any gain equal to any depreciation allowed or allowable after May 6, 1997. See *Depreciation*, later.

Separate Part of Property Used for Business

You may have used part of your property as a home and a separate part of it, such as an outbuilding, for business.

Use test not met for business part. You cannot exclude gain on the separate part of your property used for business unless you owned and lived in that part of your property for at least 2 years during the 5-year period ending on the date of the sale. If you do not meet the use test for the business part of the property, an allocation of the gain on the sale is required. For this purpose, you must allocate the basis of the property and the amount realized upon its sale between the business part and the part used as a home. You must report the sale of the business part on Form 4797.

Use test met for business part (business use in year of sale). If you used a separate part of your property for business in the year of sale, you should treat the sale of the property as the sale of two properties, even if you met the use test for the business part. You must report the sale of the business part on Form 4797.

To determine the amount to report on Form 4797, you must divide your selling price, selling expenses, and basis between the part of the property used for business and the separate part used as your home. In the same way, if you qualify to exclude any of the gain on the business part of your property, also divide your maximum exclusion between that part of the property and the separate part used as your home.

Excluding gain on the business part of your property. You generally can exclude gain on the part of your property used for business if you owned and lived in that part as your main home for at least 2 years during the 5-year period ending on the date of the sale.

Use test met for business part (no business use in year of sale). If you have used a separate part of your property for business (though not in the year of sale) but meet the use test for both the business part and the part you use as a home, you do not need to treat the transaction as the sale of two properties. Also, you do not need to file Form 4797. You generally can exclude gain on the entire property.

Depreciation

If you were entitled to deduct depreciation on the part of your home used for business, you cannot exclude the part of the gain equal to any depreciation you deducted (or could have deducted) for periods after May 6, 1997. This means that when figuring the amount of gain you can exclude, you must reduce the total gain by any depreciation allowed or allowable on the part of your home used for business after May 6, 1997.

If you can show by adequate records or other evidence that the depreciation you actually deducted (the allowed depreciation) was less than the amount you were entitled to deduct (the allowable depreciation), the amount you cannot exclude (and must subtract from your total gain when figuring your exclusion) is the amount you actually deducted.

You do not have to reduce the gain by any depreciation you deducted (or could have deducted) for a separate structure for which you cannot exclude the allocable portion of the gain.

Basis Adjustment

If you used any part of your home for business, you must adjust the basis of your home for any depreciation that was allowable for its business use, even if you did not claim it. If you deducted less depreciation than you could have under the method you properly selected, you must decrease the basis by the amount you could have deducted under that method. If you deducted more depreciation than you should have under the method you properly selected, you must decrease the basis by the amount you should have deducted, plus the part of the excess deducted that actually decreased your tax liability for any year. For more information on reducing the basis of your property for depreciation, see Publication 551.

Reporting the Sale

Do not report the 2014 sale of your main home on your tax return unless:

- You have a gain and you do not qualify to exclude all of it,

- You have a gain and choose not to exclude it, or

- You received a Form 1099-S, Proceeds from Real Estate Transactions, for the sale or exchange.

If any of these conditions apply, report the gain or loss as explained in the Instructions for Schedule D.

If you used the home for business, you may have to use Form 4797 to report the sale of the business part. See the Instructions for Form 4797.

More Information

This section covers only the basic rules for the sale or exchange of your home. For more information, see Publication 523, Selling Your Home.

Business Furniture and Equipment

This section discusses the depreciation and section 179 deductions you may be entitled to take for furniture and equipment you use in your home for business or work as an employee. These deductions are available whether or not you qualify to deduct expenses for the business use of your home.

This section explains the different rules for each of the following.

- Listed property.

- Property bought for business use.

- Personal property converted to business use.

Listed Property

If you use certain types of property, called listed property, in your home, special rules apply. Listed property includes computers and related equipment and any property of a type generally used for entertainment, recreation, and amusement (including photographic, phonographic, and video recording equipment).

Exception for certain use of computers. Computers and related equipment used exclusively in a qualifying office in your home are not listed property. If you qualify to deduct expenses for the business use of your home (see *Qualifying for a Deduction*, earlier) and you use your computer exclusively in your qualifying office in the home, do not use the listed property rules discussed in this section; instead, follow the rules discussed under *Property Bought for Business Use*, later.

More-than-50%-use test. If you bought listed property and placed it in service during the year, you must use it more than 50% for business (including work as an employee) to claim a section 179 deduction or an accelerated depreciation deduction.

If your business use of listed property is 50% or less, you cannot take a section 179 deduction and you must depreciate the property using the Alternative Depreciation System (ADS) (straight line method). For more information on ADS, see Publication 946.

Listed property meets the more-than-50%-use test for any year if its qualified business use is more than 50% of its total use. You must allocate the use of any item of listed property used for more than one purpose during the year among its various uses. You cannot use the percentage of investment use as part of the percentage of qualified business use to meet the more-than-50%-use test. However, you do use the combined total of business and investment use to figure your depreciation deduction for the property.

Example 1. Sarah does not qualify to claim a deduction for the business use of her home, but she uses her home computer 40% of the time for a business she operates out of her home. She also uses the computer 50% of the time to manage her investments. Sarah's home computer is listed property because it is not used in a qualified office in her home. She does not use the computer more than 50% for business, so she cannot elect a section 179 deduction. She can use her combined business/investment use (90%) to figure her depreciation deduction using ADS.

Example 2. If Sarah uses her computer 60% of the time for her business and 30% for managing her investments, her computer meets the more-than-50%-use test. She can elect a section 179 deduction. She can use her combined business/investment use (90%) to figure her depreciation deduction using the General Depreciation System (GDS).

Employee. If you use your own listed property (or listed property you rent) in your work as an employee, the property is business-use property only if you meet the following requirements.

- The use is for your employer's convenience.

- The use is required as a condition of your employment.

The use of property as a condition of your employment means that it is necessary for you to properly perform your work. Whether the use of the property is required for this purpose depends on all the facts and circumstances. Your employer does not have to tell you specifically to use the property. Nor is a statement by your employer to that effect sufficient.

Years following the year placed in service. If, in a year after you place an item of listed property in service, you fail to meet the more-than-50%-use test for that item of property, you may be required to do the following.

1. Figure depreciation, beginning with the year you no longer use the property more than 50% for business, using the straight line method (ADS).

2. Figure any excess depreciation (include any section 179 deduction on the property in figuring excess depreciation) and add it to:

    a. Your gross income, and

    b. The adjusted basis of your property.

For more information, see Publication 946.

Reporting and recordkeeping requirements. If you use listed property in your business, you must file Form 4562 to claim a depreciation or section 179 deduction. Begin with Part V, Section A, of that form.

 You cannot take any depreciation or section 179 deduction for the use of listed property unless you can prove your business/investment use with adequate records or sufficient evidence to support your own statements.

To meet the adequate records requirement, you must maintain an account book, diary, log, statement of expense, trip sheet, or similar record or other documentary evidence that is sufficient to establish business/investment use. For more information on what records to keep, see Publication 946.

Property Bought for Business Use

If you bought certain property during 2014 to use in your business, you can do any one of the following (subject to the limits discussed later).

- Elect a section 179 deduction for the full cost of the property.

- Depreciate the cost of the property.

- Take part of the cost as a section 179 deduction and depreciate the balance.

Section 179 Deduction

You can claim the section 179 deduction for the cost of depreciable tangible personal property bought for use in your trade or business. You can choose how much (subject to the limit) of the cost you want to deduct under section 179 and how much you want to depreciate. You can spread the section 179 deduction over several items of property in any way you choose as long as the total does not exceed the maximum allowable. You cannot take a section 179 deduction for the basis of the business part of your home.

You elect the section 179 deduction by completing Part I of Form 4562.

More information. For more information on the section 179 deduction, qualifying property, the dollar limit, and the business income limit, see Publication 946 and the Instructions for Form 4562.

Depreciation

Use Parts II and III of Form 4562 to claim your deduction for depreciation on property placed in service during the year. Do not include any costs deducted in Part I (section 179 deduction).

Most business property normally used in a home office is either 5-year or 7-year property under MACRS.

- 5-year property includes computers and peripheral equipment, typewriters, calculators, adding machines, and copiers.

- 7-year property includes office furniture and fixtures such as desks, files, and safes.

Under MACRS, you generally use the half-year convention, which allows you to deduct a half-year of depreciation in the first year you use the property in your business. If you place more than 40% of your depreciable property in service during the last 3 months of your tax year, you must use the mid-quarter convention instead of the half-year convention.

After you have determined the cost of the depreciable property (minus any section 179 deduction and special depreciation allowance taken on the property) and whether it is 5-year or 7-year property, use the table, shown next, to figure your depreciation if the half-year convention applies.

Table 4. MACRS Percentage Table for 5- and 7-Year Property Using Half-Year Convention

Recovery Year	5-Year Property	7-Year Property
1	20.00%	14.29%
2	32.00%	24.49%
3	19.20%	17.49%
4	11.52%	12.49%
5	11.52%	8.93%
6	5.76%	8.92%
7		8.93%
8		4.46%

See Publication 946 for a discussion of the mid-quarter convention and for complete MACRS percentage tables.

Example. In June 2014, Donald Kent bought a desk and three chairs for use in his office. His total bill for the furniture was $1,975. His taxable business income for the year was $3,000 without any deduction for the office furniture. Donald can elect to do one of the following.

- Take a section 179 deduction for the full cost of the office furniture.

- Take part of the cost of the furniture as a section 179 deduction and depreciate the balance.

- Depreciate the cost of the office furniture.

The furniture is 7-year property under MACRS. Donald does not take a section 179 deduction. He multiplies $1,975 by 14.29% (.1429) to get his MACRS depreciation deduction of $282.23.

Personal Property Converted to Business Use

If you use property in your home office that was used previously for personal purposes, you cannot take a section 179 deduction for the property. You also cannot take a special depreciation allowance for the property. You can depreciate it, however. The method of depreciation you use depends on when you first used the property for personal purposes.

If you began using the property for personal purposes after 1986 and change it to business use in 2014, depreciate the property under MACRS.

The basis for depreciation of property changed from personal to business use is the lesser of the following.

- The adjusted basis of the property on the date of change.

- The fair market value of the property on the date of change.

If you began using the property for personal purposes after 1980 and before 1987 and change it to business use in 2014, you generally depreciate the property under the accelerated cost recovery system (ACRS). However, if the depreciation under ACRS is greater in the first year than the depreciation under MACRS, you must depreciate it under MACRS. For information on ACRS, see Publication 534, Depreciating Property Placed in Service Before 1987.

If you began using the property for personal purposes before 1981 and change it to business use in 2014, depreciate the property by the straight line or declining balance method based on salvage value and useful life.

Recordkeeping

 You do not have to use a particular method of recordkeeping, but you must keep records that provide the information needed to figure your deductions for the business use of your home. You should keep canceled checks, receipts, and other evidence of expenses you paid.

Your records must show the following information.

- The part of your home you use for business.

- That you use part of your home exclusively and regularly for business as either your principal place of business or as the place where you meet or deal with clients or customers in the normal course of your business. (However, see the earlier discussion, *Exceptions to Exclusive Use* under *Qualifying for a Deduction.*)

- The depreciation and expenses for the business part.

You must keep your records for as long as they are important for any tax law. This is usually the later of the following dates.

- 3 years from the return due date or the date filed.

- 2 years after the tax was paid.

Keep records to prove your home's depreciable basis. This includes records of when and how you acquired your home, your original purchase price, any improvements to your home, and any depreciation you are allowed because you maintained an office in your home. You can keep copies of Forms 8829 or the Worksheet To Figure the Deduction for Business Use of Your Home, found later in this publication, as records of depreciation.

For more information on recordkeeping, see Publication 583, Starting a Business and Keeping Records.

Where To Deduct

Deduct expenses for the business use of your home on Form 1040. Where you deduct these expenses on the form depends on whether you are:

- A self-employed person, or

- An employee.

If you are a partner, see _Partners_, later, for information on where to deduct expenses for the business use of your home.

Self-Employed Persons

If you use your home in your trade or business and file Schedule C (Form 1040), report the entire deduction for business use of your home on line 30 of Schedule C (Form 1040). Whether you need to complete and attach Form 8829 to your return depends on how you figure your deduction. See _Line 30_ in the Instructions for Schedule C for more information.

If you use your home in your farming business and file Schedule F (Form 1040), report your entire deduction for business use of the home on line 32 of Schedule F (Form 1040). Enter "Business Use of Home" on the dotted line beside the entry.

Expenses deductible without regard to a business connection.

Certain expenses related to the use of your home may be deducted whether or not you use your home for business. These expenses include mortgage interest, qualified mortgage insurance premiums, real estate taxes, and casualty losses. Where you deduct these expenses depends on how you figure your deduction for business use of the home.

Using actual expenses to figure the deduction. In general, you will deduct the business portion of these expenses on Schedule C (Form 1040) or Schedule F (Form 1040) as part of your deduction for business use of your home. If you itemize your deductions, you will deduct the personal portion of these expenses on Schedule A (Form 1040).

Deductible mortgage interest. If you file Schedule C (Form 1040), enter all your deductible mortgage interest on line 10 of Form 8829. After you have figured the business part of the mortgage interest on lines 12 and 13, subtract that amount from the total on line 10. The remainder is deductible on Schedule A (Form 1040), line 10 or 11. If the interest you deduct on Schedule A (Form 1040) for your home mortgage is limited, enter the excess on line 16 of Form 8829.

If you file Schedule F (Form 1040), include the business part of your deductible home mortgage interest with your total business use of the home expenses on line 32 of Schedule F (Form 1040). Enter "Business Use of Home" on the dotted line beside the entry. You can use the Worksheet To Figure the Deduction for Business Use of Your Home, later in this publication, to figure the deductible part of mortgage interest. Enter the nonbusiness part of the deductible mortgage interest on Schedule A (Form 1040), line 10 or 11.

To determine if the limits on qualified home mortgage interest apply to you, see the Instructions for Schedule A (Form 1040) or Publication 936.

Qualified mortgage insurance premiums. If you file Schedule C (Form 1040), enter all your deductible qualified mortgage insurance premiums on line 10 of Form 8829. After you have figured the business part of the qualified mortgage insurance premiums on lines 12 and 13, subtract that amount from the qualified mortgage insurance premiums included on line 10. The remainder is deductible on Schedule A (Form 1040), line 13. If the premiums you deduct on Schedule A (Form 1040) are limited, include the excess with any excess mortgage interest and enter the total on line 16 of Form 8829.

If you file Schedule F (Form 1040), include the business part of your deductible qualified mortgage insurance premiums with your total business use of the home expenses on line 32 of Schedule F (Form 1040). Enter "Business Use of Home" on the dotted line beside the entry. You can use the Worksheet To Figure the Deduction for Business Use of Your Home, later in this publication, to figure the deductible part of qualified mortgage insurance premiums. Enter the nonbusiness part of the qualified mortgage insurance premiums on Schedule A (Form 1040), line 13.

To determine if the limits on qualified mortgage insurance premiums apply to you, see the Instructions for Schedule A (Form 1040) or Publication 936.

Real estate taxes. If you file Schedule C (Form 1040), enter all your deductible real estate taxes on Form 8829, line 11. After you have figured the business part of your taxes on lines 12 and 13, subtract that amount from your total real estate taxes on line 11. The remainder is deductible on Schedule A (Form 1040), line 6.

If you file Schedule F (Form 1040), include the business part of real estate taxes with your total business use of the home expenses on line 32 of Schedule F (Form 1040). Enter "Business Use of Home" on the dotted line beside the entry. Enter the nonbusiness part of your real estate taxes on Schedule A (Form 1040), line 6.

 If you itemize your deductions, be sure to include only the personal part of your deductible mortgage interest, qualified mortgage insurance premiums, and real estate taxes on Schedule A (Form 1040). Do not deduct any of the business part on Schedule A (Form 1040). For example, if your business percentage on Form 8829, line 7, or line 3 of the Worksheet To Figure the Deduction for Business Use of Your Home, later, is 30%, you can deduct only 70% of your deductible mortgage interest, qualified mortgage insurance premiums, and real estate taxes as personal expenses on Schedule A (Form 1040).

Casualty losses. If you are using Form 8829, refer to the specific instructions for line 9 and enter the amount from line 34 of Form 8829 on line 27 of Form 4684, Section B. Enter "See Form 8829" above line 27.

If you file Schedule F (Form 1040), enter the business part of casualty losses (line 32 of the Worksheet To Figure the Deduction for Business Use of Your Home) on line 27 of Form 4684, Section B. Attach a statement to your tax return showing how you calculated the deductible loss (you can use the worksheet as your attachment). Enter "See attached statement" above line 27.

Using the simplified method to figure your deduction. If you use the simplified method to figure your deduction for the business use of a home, your mortgage interest, qualified mortgage insurance premiums, real estate taxes, or casualty losses, subject to any limitations, are treated as personal expenses. No part of any of these expenses can be deducted as a business expense on Schedule C (Form 1040) or Schedule F (Form 1040). You can only deduct these expenses if you itemize your deductions on Schedule A (Form 1040).

Business expenses for use of your home.

Other expenses related to the use of your home may be deducted only to the extent they are related to the business use of your home. These expenses include insurance, maintenance, utilities, and depreciation of your home. You cannot deduct the personal portion of any of these expenses. Where you deduct the business portion of these expenses depends on how you figure your deduction for business use of the home.

Using actual expenses to figure your deduction. If you file Schedule C (Form 1040), report the other home expenses that would not be allowable if you did not use your home for business (for example, insurance, maintenance, utilities, and depreciation) on the appropriate lines of your Form 8829. If you rent rather than own your home, report the rent you paid on line 18 of Form 8829. If these expenses exceed the deduction limit, carry the excess over to next year. The carryover will be subject to next year's deduction limit.

If you file Schedule F (Form 1040), include your otherwise nondeductible expenses (insurance, maintenance, utilities, depreciation, etc.) with your total business use of the home expenses on Schedule F (Form 1040), line 32. Enter "Business Use of Home" on the dotted line beside the entry. If these expenses exceed the deduction limit, carry the excess over to the next year. The carryover will be subject to next year's deduction limit.

Using the simplified method to figure your deduction. You cannot deduct any of these expenses. The simplified method is an alternative to calculating and substantiating these expenses. Figure your deduction using the Simplified Method Worksheet.

Business expenses not for use of your home.

No matter how you figure the deduction for business use of your home, deduct in full your business expenses that are not for the use of your home itself (dues, salaries, supplies, certain telephone expenses, depreciation of equipment, etc.) on the appropriate lines of Schedule C (Form 1040) or Schedule F (Form 1040). These expenses are not for the use of your home, so they are not subject to the deduction limit for business use of the home expenses.

Employees

As an employee, you must itemize deductions on Schedule A (Form 1040) to claim a deduction for the business use of your home and any other employee business expenses. This generally applies to all employees, including outside salespersons. If you are a statutory employee, use Schedule C (Form 1040) to claim the expenses. Follow the instructions given earlier under _Self-Employed Persons_. The statutory employee box within box 13 on your Form W-2, Wage and Tax Statement, will be checked if you are a statutory employee.

If you have employee expenses for which you were not reimbursed, report them on Schedule A (Form 1040), line 21. You also generally must complete Form 2106 if either of the following apply.

- You claim any job-related vehicle, travel, transportation, meal, or entertainment expenses.

- Your employer paid you for any of your job expenses reportable on line 21 of Schedule A (Form 1040). (Amounts your employer included in box 1 of your Form W-2 are not considered paid by your employer.)

However, you can use the simpler Form 2106-EZ, instead of Form 2106, if you meet the following requirements.

- You were not reimbursed for your expenses by your employer, or if you were reimbursed, the reimbursement was included in box 1 of your Form W-2.

- If you claim car expenses, you use the standard mileage rate.

When your employer pays for your expenses using a reimbursement or allowance arrangement, the payments generally should not be on your Form W-2 if all the following rules for an accountable plan are met.

- You adequately account to your employer for the expenses within a reasonable period of time.

- You return any payments not spent for business expenses (excess reimbursements) within a reasonable period of time.

- You must have paid or incurred deductible expenses while performing services as an employee.

If you meet the accountable plan rules and your business expenses equal your reimbursement, do not report the reimbursement as income and do not deduct the expenses.

Adequately accounting to employer. You adequately account to your employer when you give your employer documentary evidence of your travel, mileage, and other employee business expenses, such as receipts, along with an account book, diary, or similar record in which you entered each expense at or near the time you had it.

You also may be treated as adequately accounting to your employer if your employer gives you a per diem or car allowance similar in form to, and not more than, the federal rate and you verify the time, place, and business purpose of each expense. For more information, see Publication 463 and the Instructions for Form 2106.

Deductible mortgage interest. Although you generally deduct expenses for the business use of your home on Schedule A (Form 1040), line 21, do not include any deductible home mortgage interest on that line. Instead, deduct both the business and nonbusiness parts of this interest on line 10 or 11 of Schedule A (Form 1040).

If the home mortgage interest you can deduct on lines 10 or 11 is limited by the home mortgage interest rules, you cannot deduct the excess as an employee business expense on Schedule A (Form 1040), line 21, even though you use part of your home for business. To determine if the limits on home mortgage interest apply to you, see Publication 936 or the Instructions for Schedule A (Form 1040).

Qualified mortgage insurance premiums. Although you generally deduct expenses for the business use of your home on Schedule A (Form 1040), line 21, do not include any deductible qualified mortgage insurance premiums on that line. Instead, deduct both the business and nonbusiness parts of these premiums on Schedule A (Form 1040), line 13.

If the qualified mortgage insurance premiums you can deduct on line 13 is limited, you cannot deduct the excess as an employee business expense on Schedule A (Form 1040), line 21, even though you use part of your home for business. To determine if you can deduct mortgage insurance premiums and if any limits apply to you, see Publication 936 and *Line 13* in the Instructions for Schedule A (Form 1040).

Real estate taxes. Deduct both the business and nonbusiness parts of your real estate taxes on line 6 of Schedule A (Form 1040). For more information on amounts allowable as a deduction for real estate taxes, see Publication 530.

Casualty losses. Enter the business part of casualty losses (line 32 of the Worksheet To Figure the Deduction for Business Use of Your Home, later) on Form 4684, Section B, line 27. Attach a statement to your tax return showing how you calculated the deductible loss (you can use the worksheet as your attachment). Enter "See attached statement" above line 27.

Other expenses. If you file Form 2106 or Form 2106-EZ, report on line 4 the following expenses.

- The business part of your otherwise nondeductible expenses (utilities, maintenance, insurance, depreciation of your home, etc.) that do not exceed the deduction limit or, if you elect to use the simplified method, the amount from line 5 of the Simplified Method Worksheet.

- The employee business expenses not related to the use of your home, such as advertising.

Add these to your other employee business expenses and complete the rest of the form. Enter the total from Form 2106, or Form 2106-EZ, on Schedule A (Form 1040),

line 21, where it is subject to the 2%-of-adjusted-gross-income limit. If you do not have to file Form 2106 or Form 2106-EZ, enter your total expenses directly on Schedule A (Form 1040), line 21.

Example 1. You are an employee who works at home for the convenience of your employer. You meet all the requirements to deduct expenses for the business use of your home. Your employer does not reimburse you for any of your business expenses and you are not otherwise required to file Form 2106 or Form 2106-EZ. You use actual expenses to figure the deduction for business use of your home.

As an employee, you do not have gross receipts, cost of goods sold, etc. You begin with gross income from the business use of your home, which you determine to be $6,000.

The percentage of expenses due to the business use of your home is 20%. You have the following expenses.

Deductible mortgage interest (20%)	$1,500
Real estate taxes (20%)	1,000
Total	$2,500
Expenses not related to business use of the home (100%):	
Supplies	$500
Advertising	1,300
Telephone	200
Total	$2,000
Otherwise nondeductible expenses:	
Maintenance (20%)	$200
Utilities (20%)	350
Insurance (20%)	250
Total	$800
Depreciation (20%)	$1,600

Based on the above expenses, you figure your deduction limit as follows.

Gross income		$6,000
Less:		
Deductible mortgage interest (20%)	$1,500	
Real estate taxes (20%)	1,000	
Expenses not related to business use of the home (100%)	2,000	4,500
Deduction limit		**$1,500**

Your deduction for otherwise nondeductible expenses and depreciation is limited to $1,500. You can deduct all your otherwise nondeductible expenses ($800) and $700 ($1,500 – $800) of your depreciation.

You deduct your expenses for business use of your home on Schedule A (Form 1040) as shown in the following table.

Expense	Amount	Schedule A
Deductible mortgage interest	$1,500	Line 10 or 11*
Real estate taxes	$1,000	Line 6*
Expenses not related to the business use of the home	$2,000	Line 21**
Otherwise nondeductible expenses	$800	Line 21**
Depreciation	$700	Line 21**

*In addition to the 80% nonbusiness part of the expense.

**Subject to the 2%-of-adjusted-gross-income limit.

You can carry over the $900 ($1,600 – $700) of depreciation that exceeds the deduction limit to the next year in which you use actual expenses, subject to the deduction limit for that year.

Example 2. The facts are the same as *Example 1* except that you elect to use the simplified method to figure the deduction for the business use of your home. You used 400 square feet of your home for work during the entire year. You did not share the space with any other qualified business use of your home.

Your gross income limitation is $4,000. This is the difference between the gross income related to the use of your home ($6,000) and the expenses that are not related to the business use of your home ($2,000).

Using the simplified method, you may claim a deduction for a maximum of 300 square feet. The deduction for business use of your home is the lesser of $1,500 (300 square feet × $5) or your gross income limitation. You include your deduction for business use of the home ($1,500) and your expenses that are not related to the business use of your home ($2,000) on line 21 of your Schedule A. These amounts are still subject to the 2%-of-adjusted-gross-income limit.

You will treat the business portion of your mortgage interest and real estate taxes as personal expenses when figuring the amount to include on lines 6 and 10 (or 11) of your Schedule A.

The depreciation of the part of your home used for business is deemed to be zero and you will not have a carryover of any expenses.

Partners

You may be allowed to deduct unreimbursed ordinary and necessary expenses you paid on behalf of the partnership (including qualified expenses for the business use of your home) if you were required to pay these expenses under the partnership agreement.

If you are using actual expenses to figure your deduction for the business use of your home, use the Worksheet To Figure the Deduction for Business Use of Your Home, later. If you are using the simplified method to figure your deduction for the business use of your home, use the Simplified Method Worksheet, later.

Deducting unreimbursed partnership expenses. See the following forms and related instructions for information about deducting unreimbursed partnership expenses.

- Schedule E (Form 1040), Supplemental Income and Loss.
- Schedule SE (Form 1040), Self-Employment Tax.
- Schedule K-1 (Form 1065), Partner's Share of Income, Deductions, Credits, etc.

More information. For more information about partners and partnerships, see Publication 541, Partnerships.

Worksheet To Figure the Deduction for Business Use of Your Home

This worksheet is to be used by taxpayers filing Schedule F (Form 1040) or who are employees or partners, and who are using actual expenses to figure the deduction. If you are using the simplified method to figure your deduction, use the Simplified Method Worksheet, later.

Instructions for the Worksheet

The Worksheet To Figure the Deduction for Business Use of Your Home is to be used by taxpayers filing Schedule F (Form 1040) or who are employees or partners, and who are using actual expenses to figure the deduction. The following instructions explain how to complete each part of the worksheet.

Partners. See *Partners* under *Where To Deduct*, earlier, before completing the worksheet.

 If you file Schedule C (Form 1040) and use actual expenses to figure your deduction, use Form 8829 to figure the deductions and attach the form to your return.

Part 1—Part of Your Home Used for Business

Lines 1-3. If you figure the percentage based on area, use lines 1 through 3 to figure the business-use percentage. Enter the percentage on line 3.

You can use any other reasonable method that accurately reflects your business-use percentage. If you operate a daycare facility and you meet the exception to the exclusive use test for part or all of the area you use for business, you must figure the business-use percentage for that area as explained under *Daycare Facility*, earlier. If you use another method to figure your business percentage, skip lines 1 and 2 and enter the percentage on line 3.

Worksheet To Figure the Deduction for Business Use of Your Home

Keep for Your Records

Use this worksheet if you file Schedule F (Form 1040) or you are an employee or a partner, and you are using actual expenses to figure your deduction for business use of the home. Use a separate worksheet for each qualified business use of your home.

PART 1—Part of Your Home Used for Business:

1)	Area of home used for business	1) _____
2)	Total area of home	2) _____
3)	Percentage of home used for business (divide line 1 by line 2 and show result as percentage)	3) _____ %

PART 2—Figure Your Allowable Deduction

4)	Gross income from business (see instructions)	4) _____

		(a) Direct Expenses	(b) Indirect Expenses
5)	Casualty losses	5) _____	_____
6)	Deductible mortgage interest and qualified mortgage insurance premiums	6) _____	_____
7)	Real estate taxes	7) _____	_____
8)	Total of lines 5 through 7	8) _____	_____

9)	Multiply line 8, column (b), by line 3	9) _____
10)	Add line 8, column (a), and line 9	10) _____
11)	Business expenses not from business use of home (see instructions)	11) _____
12)	Add lines 10 and 11	12) _____
13)	Deduction limit. Subtract line 12 from line 4	13) _____

		(a) Direct Expenses	(b) Indirect Expenses
14)	Excess mortgage interest and qualified mortgage insurance premiums	14) _____	_____
15)	Insurance	15) _____	_____
16)	Rent	16) _____	_____
17)	Repairs and maintenance	17) _____	_____
18)	Utilities	18) _____	_____
19)	Other expenses	19) _____	_____
20)	Add lines 14 through 19	20) _____	_____

21)	Multiply line 20, column (b) by line 3	21) _____
22)	Carryover of operating expenses from prior year (see instructions)	22) _____
23)	Add line 20, column (a), line 21, and line 22	23) _____
24)	Allowable operating expenses. Enter the **smaller** of line 13 or line 23	24) _____
25)	Limit on excess casualty losses and depreciation. Subtract line 24 from line 13	25) _____
26)	Excess casualty losses (see instructions)	26) _____
27)	Depreciation of your home from line 39 below	27) _____
28)	Carryover of excess casualty losses and depreciation from prior year (see instructions)	28) _____
29)	Add lines 26 through 28	29) _____
30)	Allowable excess casualty losses and depreciation. Enter the **smaller** of line 25 or line 29	30) _____
31)	Add lines 10, 24, and 30	31) _____
32)	Casualty losses included on lines 10 and 30 (see instructions)	32) _____
33)	Allowable expenses for business use of your home. (Subtract line 32 from line 31.) See instructions for where to enter on your return	33) _____

PART 3—Depreciation of Your Home

34)	Smaller of adjusted basis or fair market value of home (see instructions)	34) _____
35)	Basis of land	35) _____
36)	Basis of building (subtract line 35 from line 34)	36) _____
37)	Business basis of building (multiply line 36 by line 3)	37) _____
38)	Depreciation percentage (from applicable table or method)	38) _____ %
39)	Depreciation allowable (multiply line 37 by line 38)	39) _____

PART 4—Carryover of Unallowed Expenses to Next Year

40)	Operating expenses. Subtract line 24 from line 23. If less than zero, enter -0-	40) _____
41)	Excess casualty losses and depreciation. Subtract line 30 from line 29. If less than zero, enter -0-	41) _____

Part 2—Figure Your Allowable Deduction

Line 4. If you file Schedule F (Form 1040), enter your total gross income that is related to the business use of your home. This generally would be the amount on line 9 of Schedule F (Form 1040).

If you are an employee, enter your total wages that are related to the business use of your home.

Lines 5-7. Enter only the amounts that would be deductible whether or not you used your home for business (that is, amounts allowable as itemized deductions on Schedule A (Form 1040)).

Generally (disaster) waivers include only the part of a casualty loss that exceeds $100 plus 10% of adjusted gross income.

If you file Schedule F (Form 1040) or are a partner, treat qualified mortgage insurance premiums as personal expenses for this step. Figure the amount to include on line 6 by completing Schedule A (Form 1040), line 13, in accordance with the instructions for line 13 in the Instructions for Schedule A (Form 1040). However, when figuring your adjusted gross income (Form 1040, line 38) for this purpose, exclude the gross income from business use of your home and the deductions attributable to that income. Include on line 6 the amount from Schedule A (Form 1040), line 13. See *Lines 14–22*, later, to deduct part of the qualified mortgage insurance premiums not allowed because of the adjusted gross income limit. Do not file or use that Schedule A (Form 1040) to figure the amount to deduct on line 13 of that schedule. Instead, complete a separate Schedule A (Form 1040) to deduct the personal portion of your qualified mortgage insurance premiums.

Under column (a), *Direct Expenses*, enter expenses that benefit only the business part of your home. Under column (b), *Indirect Expenses*, enter expenses that benefit the entire home. You generally enter 100% of the expense. However, if the business percentage of an indirect expense is different from the percentage on line 3, enter only the business part of the expense on the appropriate line in column (a), and leave that line in column (b) blank.

Lines 9-10. Multiply your total indirect expenses (line 8, column (b)) by the business percentage from line 3. Enter the result on line 9. Add this amount to the total direct expenses (line 8, column (a)) and enter the total on line 10.

Lines 11-13. Enter any other business expenses that are not attributable to business use of the home on line 11. For employees, examples include travel, supplies, and business telephone expenses. Farmers generally should enter their total farm expenses before deducting office-in-the-home expenses. Do not enter the deductible part of your self-employment tax. Add the amounts on lines 10 and 11, and enter the total on line 12. Subtract line 12 from line 4, and enter the result on line 13. This is your deduction limit. You use it to determine whether you can deduct any of your other expenses for business use of the home this year. If you cannot, you will carry them over to the next year in which you use actual expenses to figure the deduction.

If line 13 is zero or less, enter zero. Deduct your expenses for deductible home mortgage interest, qualified mortgage insurance premiums, real estate taxes, casualty losses, and any business expenses not attributable to use of your home on the appropriate lines of the schedule(s) for Form 1040 as explained earlier under *Where To Deduct*.

Lines 14-22. On lines 14 through 19, enter your otherwise nondeductible expenses for the business use of your home. These include utilities, insurance, repairs, and maintenance. If you rent, report the amount paid on line 16. If you file Schedule F (Form 1040), include any part of your home mortgage interest or qualified mortgage insurance premiums that is more than the limits given in Publication 936. (If you are an employee, do not enter any excess home mortgage interest or qualified mortgage insurance premiums.) In column (a), enter the expenses that benefit only the business part of your home (direct expenses). In column (b), enter the expenses that benefit the entire home (indirect expenses). Multiply line 20, column (b) by the business-use percentage (line 3) and enter this amount on line 21.

If you deducted actual expenses for the business use of your home on your 2013 tax return, enter on line 22 the amount from line 40 of your 2013 worksheet. If you used the simplified method in 2013, enter on line 22 the amount from line 6a of your 2013 Simplified Method Worksheet.

Lines 25-30. On lines 25 through 30, figure your limit on deductions for excess casualty losses and depreciation.

On line 26, figure the excess casualty loss by multiplying the business use percentage from line 3 by the part of casualty losses that would not be allowable if you did not use your home for business (that is, the casualty losses in excess of the amount on line 5).

On line 27, enter the depreciation deduction from Part 3.

If you deducted actual expenses for business use of your home on your 2013 tax return, enter on line 28 the amount from line 41 of your 2013 worksheet. If you used the simplified method in 2013, enter on line 28 the amount from line 6b of your 2013 Simplified Method Worksheet.

On lines 29 and 30, figure your allowable excess casualty losses and depreciation.

Lines 31-33. On line 31, total all allowable business use of the home deductions.

On line 32, enter the total of the casualty losses shown on lines 10 and 30. Enter the amount from line 32 on line 27 of Form 4684, Section B. Attach a statement to your tax return showing how you calculated the deductible loss (you can use the worksheet as your attachment) and enter "See attached statement" above line 27 of Form 4684. See the Instructions for Form 4684 for more information on completing that form.

Line 33 is the total (other than casualty losses) allowable as a deduction for business use of your home. If you file Schedule F (Form 1040), enter this amount on line 32, Other expenses, of Schedule F (Form 1040) and enter "Business Use of Home" on the line beside the entry. Do not add the specific expenses into other line totals of Part II of Schedule F (Form 1040).

If you are an employee or partner, see *Where To Deduct*, earlier, for information on how to claim the deduction.

Part 3—Depreciation of Your Home

Figure your depreciation deduction on lines 34 through 39. On line 34, enter the smaller of the adjusted basis or the fair market value of the property at the time you first used it for business. Do not adjust this amount for changes in basis or value after that date. Allocate the basis between the land and the building on lines 35 and 36. You cannot depreciate any part of the land. On line 38, enter the correct percentage for the current year from the tables in Publication 946. Multiply this percentage by the business basis to get the depreciation deduction. Enter this figure on lines 39 and 27. Complete and attach Form 4562 to your return if this is the first year you used your home, or an improvement or addition to your home, in business.

Part 4—Carryover of Unallowed Expenses to Next Year

Complete these lines to figure the expenses that must be carried forward to the next year in which you use actual expenses.

Worksheets To Figure the Deduction for Business Use of Your Home (Simplified Method)

The Simplified Method Worksheet and the Daycare Facility Worksheet in this section are to be used by taxpayers filing Schedule F (Form 1040) or who are employees or partners, and who are using the simplified method to figure the deduction. If you are filing Schedule C (Form 1040) to report a business use of your home in your trade or business and you are using the simplified method to figure the deduction, use the Simplified Method Worksheet and Daycare Facility Worksheet in your Instructions for Schedule C for that business use.

The Area Adjustment Worksheet in this section may be used by any taxpayer using the simplified method to figure the deduction.

Simplified Method Worksheet

Use this worksheet if you file Schedule F (Form 1040) or you are an employee or a partner, and you are using the simplified method to figure your deduction for business use of the home. Use a separate worksheet for each qualified business use of your home.

1. Enter the amount of the gross income limitation. See Instructions for the Simplified Method Worksheet	1. _____
2. Allowable square footage for the qualified business use. Do not enter more than 300 square feet. See Instructions for the Simplified Method Worksheet	2. _____
3. Simplified method amount	
a. Maximum allowable amount	3a. ___$5___
b. For daycare facilities not used exclusively for business, enter the decimal amount from the Daycare Facility Worksheet; otherwise, enter 1.0	3b. _____
c. Multiply line 3a by line 3b and enter result to 2 decimal places	3c. _____
4. Multiply line 2 by line 3c	4. _____
5. **Allowable expenses using the simplified method.** Enter the smaller of line 1 or line 4. If zero or less, enter -0-. See *Where To Deduct*, earlier, for where to enter this amount on your return	5. _____
6. **Carryover of unallowed expenses from 2013 that are not allowed in 2014.**	
a. Operating expenses. Enter the amount, if any, from your 2013 Worksheet To Figure the Deduction for Business Use of Your Home, line 40	6a. _____
b. Excess casualty losses and depreciation. Enter the amount, if any, from your 2013 Worksheet To Figure the Deduction for Business Use of Your Home, line 41	6b. _____

Daycare Facility Worksheet (for simplified method)

1. Multiply days used for daycare during the year by hours used per day .... 1. _____

2. Total hours available for use during the year. See Instructions for the Daycare Facility
   Worksheet .... 2. _____

3. Divide line 1 by line 2. Enter the result as a decimal amount here and on line 3b of the
   Simplified Method Worksheet .... 3. _____

Instructions for the Simplified Method Worksheet

If you are an employee or a partner, or you file Schedule F (Form 1040), and you elected to use the simplified method, use the Simplified Method Worksheet. The following instructions explain how to complete this worksheet.

Partners. See *Partners* under *Where To Deduct*, earlier, before completing the Simplified Method Worksheet.

Use the Simplified Method Worksheet to figure the amount of expenses you may deduct for a qualified business use of a home if you are electing to use the simplified method for that home. If you are not electing to use the simplified method, use Form 8829 or the Worksheet to Figure the Deduction for Business Use of Your Home, earlier, as appropriate.

Line 1. If all gross income from your trade or business is from this qualified business use of your home, figure your gross income limitation as follows.

A. Enter the amount of gross income. If you file Schedule F (Form 1040), this amount would generally be the amount on line 9 of Schedule F. If you are an employee, your gross income is your wages related to the business use of your home . . . . _____

B. Enter any gain derived from the business use of your home and shown on Form 8949 (and included on Schedule D) or Form 4797 . . . . _____

C. Add lines A and B . . . . _____

D. Business expenses not from business use of the home. . . . . _____

E. Enter the loss (as a positive number) shown on Form 8949 (and included on Schedule D) or Form 4797 that are allocable to the business, but not allocable to the use of the home . . . . _____

F. Add lines D and E . . . . _____

G. Gross income limitation. Subtract line F from line C. Enter the result here and on line 1 . . . . _____

If some of the income is from a place of business other than your home, you must first determine the part of your gross income from the business use of your home. In making this determination, consider the amount of time you spend at each location as well as other facts. After determining the part of your gross income from the business use of your home, subtract from that amount the total expenses and any losses that are allocable to the business in which you use your home but that are not allocable to the use of the home.

Only include on line A the gross income from the business that is related to the business use of your home. Only include on line D and line E the deductible business expenses and losses that are related to the business activity in the home, but not related to the use of the home itself.

Note. If you had more than one home in which you conducted this business during the year, include only the income earned and the deductions attributable to that income during the period you owned the home for which you elected to use the simplified method.

Line 2. If you used the same area for the entire year, enter the smaller of the square feet you actually used or 300. If you and your spouse conducted the business as a qualified joint venture, split the square feet between you and your spouse in the same manner you split your other tax attributes. If you shared space with someone else, used the home for business for only part of the year, or the area you used changed during the year, see *Allowable area* under *Using the Simplified Method*, earlier, before entering an amount on this line. Do not enter more than 300 square feet or, if applicable, the average monthly allowable square footage on this line. See Part-year use or area changes (for simplified method only) for more information on how to figure your average monthly allowable square footage.

Line 3b. If your qualified business use is providing daycare, you may need to account for the time that you used the same part of your home for other purposes. If you used the part of your home exclusively and regularly for providing daycare, enter 1.0 on line 3b. If you did not use the part of your home exclusively for providing daycare, complete the Daycare Facility Worksheet to figure what number to enter on line 3b.

Line 6. Since you are using the simplified method this year, you cannot deduct the amounts you entered on lines 6a and 6b this year. If you figure your deduction for business use of the home using actual expenses next year, you will be able to include these expenses when you figure your deduction.

Instructions for the Daycare Facility Worksheet

Use the Daycare Facility Worksheet to figure the percentage to use on line 3b of the Simplified Method Worksheet. If you do not use the area of your home exclusively for

Area Adjustment Worksheet (for simplified method)

If you used the same area for your qualified business use for the entire year, complete only Part I; otherwise skip Part I, and complete Part II using lines 1 through 5 to help you figure the amount to enter for each month. All amounts reported on this worksheet must be in square feet.

Part I. Same area was used for the entire year.

1. Area used for this qualified business use. . . . . **1.** _____

2. Shared use. Complete line 2 if someone else also used the home to conduct business that qualifies for the deduction; otherwise, enter 300 on line 2d and go to line 3.

   a. Area not shared. Enter portion of line 1 that was not shared with another person's qualified business use of the home . . . . **2a.** _____

   b. Total area shared with another person's qualified business use. Subtract line 2a from line 1 . . . . . **2b.** _____

   c. Reasonable allocation of shared area to this qualified business use . . . . **2c.** _____

   d. Add lines 2a and 2c . . . . **2d.** _____

3. Multiple qualified business uses. Complete line 3 if you used the home for more than one qualified business use; otherwise, enter 300 on line 3d and go to line 4.

   a. Total area of home used for all your qualified business uses . . . . **3a.** _____

   b. Maximum area . . . . **3b.** _____ 300 _____

   c. Enter the smaller of line 3a and 3b . . . . **3c.** _____

   d. Reasonable allocation of line 3c to this qualified business use . . . . **3d.** _____

4. Maximum area . . . . **4.** _____ 300 _____

5. Enter the smaller of lines 1, 2d, 3d, and 4. Enter the result on line 2 of the Simplified Method Worksheet . . . . **5.** _____

Part II. Area changed during the year or was used for only part of the year.

6. Complete lines 6a through 6n if you used the area for this qualified business use for part of the year or the area used for this qualifying business use changed during the year.

	(i) Month	**Note.** If your qualified business use was less than 15 days in a month, enter -0- in column (ii) for that month; otherwise, use lines 1 through 5 above for each month, and enter the amount you get for line 5 in column (ii) for that month.	(ii) Area
a.	January	. . . .	
b.	February	. . . .	
c.	March	. . . .	
d.	April	. . . .	
e.	May	. . . .	
f.	June	. . . .	
g.	July	. . . .	
h.	August	. . . .	
i.	September	. . . .	
j.	October	. . . .	
k.	November	. . . .	
l.	December	. . . .	

   m. Add lines 6a through 6l, column (ii) . . . . **6m.** _____

   n. Average monthly allowable square footage. Divide line 6m by 12. Enter the result on line 2 of the Simplified Method Worksheet. . . . . **6n.** _____

daycare, you must reduce the amount on line 3a before figuring your deduction using the simplified method.

⬤ *If you used at least 300 square feet for daycare regularly and exclusively during the year, then you do not need to complete this worksheet. This worksheet is only needed if you did not use the allowable area exclusively for daycare.*

Line 1. Enter the total number of hours the facility was used for daycare during the year.

Example. Your home is used Monday through Friday for 12 hours per day for 250 days during the year. It is also used on 50 Saturdays for 8 hours a day. Enter 3,400 hours on line 4 (3,000 hours for weekdays plus 400 hours for Saturdays).

Line 2. If you used your home for daycare during the entire year, multiply 365 days (366 for a leap year) by 24 hours, and enter the result.

If you started or stopped using your home for daycare during the year, you must prorate the number of hours based on the number of days the home was available for daycare. Multiply 24 hours by the number of days available and enter that result.

Instructions for the Area Adjustment Worksheet

Use the Area Adjustment Worksheet to figure the area that you may use to figure your deduction.

Line 2. If you and another person both used the home to conduct business that qualifies for the deduction, the same area cannot be used by both persons to figure the deduction.

Line 2c. With the other people using the home for qualified business use, determine a reasonable allocation of shared space to your qualified business use. Do not include area that is claimed by another person.

Line 3. If you used your home for more than one qualified business use, the total area that you can use to figure the deduction is still only 300 square feet, not 300 square feet per business use. You may allocate the square footage among your qualified business uses in any reasonable manner, but you may not allocate more square feet to a qualified business use than was actually used.

Line 3d. Allocate part of line 3c to this qualified business use. Do not allocate more square feet to this qualified business use than was actually used during the year. Do not allocate any part of line 3c to this qualified business use that you allocated to another qualified business use.

Line 6. If you only used the area for this qualified business use for part of the year or the area used for this qualifying business use changed during the year, then you need to figure the average monthly allowable square footage. To do this, use lines 1 through 5 of this worksheet for each month. For example, for January, complete lines 1 through 5 using the area and allocation information for January only; then, enter the result in line 6a, column (ii). If, in any month, you did not have 15 or more days of this qualified business use, enter -0- for that month. For example, if you did not begin using your home for this qualified business use until January 20, enter -0- in line 6a, column (ii).

How To Get Tax Help

Do you need help with a tax issue or preparing your tax return, or do you need a free publication or form?

Preparing and filing your tax return. Find free options to prepare and file your return on IRS.gov or in your local community if you qualify.

- Go to IRS.gov and click on the Filing tab to see your options.
- Enter "Free File" in the search box to use brand name software to prepare and *e-file* your federal tax return for free.
- Enter "VITA" in the search box, download the free IRS2Go app, or call 1-800-906-9887 to find the nearest Volunteer Income Tax Assistance or Tax Counseling for the Elderly (TCE) location for free tax preparation.
- Enter "TCE" in the search box, download the free IRS2Go app, or call 1-888-227-7669 to find the nearest Tax Counseling for the Elderly location for free tax preparation.

The Volunteer Income Tax Assistance (VITA) program offers free tax help to people who generally make $53,000 or less, persons with disabilities, the elderly, and limited-English-speaking taxpayers who need help preparing their own tax returns. The Tax Counseling for the Elderly (TCE) program offers free tax help for all taxpayers, particularly those who are 60 years of age and older. TCE volunteers specialize in answering questions about pensions and retirement-related issues unique to seniors.

Getting answers to your tax law questions. IRS.gov and IRS2Go are ready when you are—24 hours a day, 7 days a week.

- Enter "ITA" in the search box on IRS.gov for the Interactive Tax Assistant, a tool that will ask you questions on a number of tax law topics and provide answers. You can print the entire interview and the final response.
- Enter "Tax Map" or "Tax Trails" in the search box for detailed information by tax topic.
- Enter "Pub 17" in the search box to get Pub. 17, Your Federal Income Tax for Individuals, which features details on tax-saving opportunities, 2014 tax changes, and thousands of interactive links to help you find answers to your questions.
- Call TeleTax at 1-800-829-4477 for recorded information on a variety of tax topics.

- Access tax law information in your electronic filing software.

- Go to IRS.gov and click on the Help & Resources tab for more information.

Tax forms and publications. You can download or print all of the forms and publications you may need on *www.irs.gov/formspubs*. Otherwise, you can:

- Go to *www.irs.gov/orderforms* to place an order and have forms mailed to you, or

- Call 1-800-829-3676 to order current-year forms, instructions, publications, and prior-year forms and instructions (limited to 5 years).

You should receive your order within 10 business days.

Where to file your tax return.

- There are many ways to file your return electronically. It's safe, quick and easy. See *Preparing and filing your tax return*, earlier, for more information.

- See your tax return instructions to determine where to mail your completed paper tax return.

Getting a transcript or copy of a return.

- Go to IRS.gov and click on "Get Transcript of Your Tax Records" under "Tools."

- Download the free IRS2Go app to your smart phone and use it to order transcripts of your tax returns or tax account.

- Call the transcript toll-free line at 1-800-908-9946.

- Mail Form 4506-T or Form 4506T-EZ (both available on IRS.gov).

Using online tools to help prepare your return. Go to IRS.gov and click on the Tools bar to use these and other self-service options.

- The *Earned Income Tax Credit Assistant* determines if you are eligible for the EIC.

- The *First Time Homebuyer Credit Account Look-up* tool provides information on your repayments and account balance.

- The *Alternative Minimum Tax (AMT) Assistant* determines whether you may be subject to AMT.

- The *Online EIN Application* helps you get an Employer Identification Number.

- The *IRS Withholding Calculator* estimates the amount you should have withheld from your paycheck for federal income tax purposes.

- The *Electronic Filing PIN Request* helps to verify your identity when you do not have your prior year AGI or prior year self-selected PIN available.

Understanding identity theft issues.

- Go to *www.irs.gov/uac/Identity-Protection* for information and videos.

- If your SSN has been lost or stolen or you suspect you are a victim of tax-related identity theft, visit *www.irs.gov/identitytheft* to learn what steps you should take.

Checking on the status of a refund.

- Go to *www.irs.gov/refunds*.

- Download the free IRS2Go app to your smart phone and use it to check your refund status.

- Call the automated refund hotline at 1-800-829-1954.

Making a tax payment. You can make electronic payments online, by phone, or from a mobile device. Paying electronically is safe and secure. The IRS uses the latest encryption technology and does not store banking information. It's easy and secure and much quicker than mailing in a check or money order. Go to IRS.gov and click on the Payments tab or the "Pay Your Tax Bill" icon to make a payment using the following options.

- *Direct Pay* (only if you are an individual who has a checking or savings account).

- Debit or credit card.

- Electronic Federal Tax Payment System.

- Check or money order.

What if I can't pay now? Click on the Payments tab or the "Pay Your Tax Bill" icon on IRS.gov to find more information about these additional options.

- An *online payment agreement* determines if you are eligible to apply for an installment agreement if you cannot pay your taxes in full today. With the needed information, you can complete the application in about 30 minutes, and get immediate approval.

- An offer in compromise allows you to settle your tax debt for less than the full amount you owe. Use the *Offer in Compromise Pre-Qualifier* to confirm your eligibility.

Checking the status of an amended return. Go to IRS.gov and click on the Tools tab and then *Where's My Amended Return?*

Understanding an IRS notice or letter. Enter "Understanding your notice" in the search box on IRS.gov to find additional information about your IRS notice or letter.

Visiting the IRS. Locate the nearest Taxpayer Assistance Center using the Office Locator tool on IRS.gov. Enter "office locator" in the search box. Or choose the "Contact Us" option on the IRS2Go app and search Local Offices. Before you visit, use the Locator tool to check hours and services available.

Watching IRS videos. The IRS Video portal *www.irsvideos.gov* contains video and audio presentations on topics of interest to individuals, small businesses, and tax professionals. You'll find video clips of tax topics, archived versions of live panel discussions and Webinars, and audio archives of tax practitioner phone forums.

Getting tax information in other languages. For taxpayers whose native language is not English, we have the following resources available.

1. Taxpayers can find information on IRS.gov in the following languages.

   a. *Spanish*.

   b. *Chinese*.

   c. *Vietnamese*.

   d. *Korean*.

   e. *Russian*.

2. The IRS Taxpayer Assistance Centers provide over-the-phone interpreter service in over 170 languages, and the service is available free to taxpayers.

The Taxpayer Advocate Service Is Here To Help You

What is the Taxpayer Advocate Service?

The Taxpayer Advocate Service (TAS) is an **independent** organization within the Internal Revenue Service that helps taxpayers and protects taxpayer rights. Our job is to ensure that every taxpayer is treated fairly and that you know and understand your rights under the *Taxpayer Bill of Rights*.

What Can the Taxpayer Advocate Service Do For You?

We can help you resolve problems that you can't resolve with the IRS. And our service is free. If you qualify for our assistance, you will be assigned to one advocate who will work with you throughout the process and will do everything possible to resolve your issue. TAS can help you if:

- Your problem is causing financial difficulty for you, your family, or your business,

- You face (or your business is facing) an immediate threat of adverse action, or

- You've tried repeatedly to contact the IRS but no one has responded, or the IRS hasn't responded by the date promised.

How Can You Reach Us?

We have offices *in every state, the District of Columbia, and Puerto Rico*. Your local advocate's number is in your local directory and at *www.taxpayeradvocate.irs.gov*. You can also call us at 1-877-777-4778.

How Can You Learn About Your Taxpayer Rights?

The Taxpayer Bill of Rights describes ten basic rights that all taxpayers have when dealing with the IRS. Our Tax Toolkit at *www.taxpayeradvocate.irs.gov* can help you understand *what these rights mean to you* and how they apply. These are *your* rights. Know them. Use them.

How Else Does the Taxpayer Advocate Service Help Taxpayers?

TAS works to resolve large-scale problems that affect many taxpayers. If you know of one of these broad issues, please report it to us at *www.irs.gov/sams*.

Low Income Taxpayer Clinics

Low Income Taxpayer Clinics (LITCs) serve individuals whose income is below a certain level and need to resolve tax problems such as audits, appeals, and tax collection disputes. Some clinics can provide information about taxpayer rights and responsibilities in different languages for individuals who speak English as a second language. To find a clinic near you, visit *www.irs.gov/litc* or see IRS Publication 4134, *Low Income Taxpayer Clinic List*.

∎

Exhibit A. **Family Daycare Provider Meal and Snack Log**

Name of Provider _____

Week of _____ Year _____

Keep For Your Records

Child's Name	Monday	Tuesday	Wednesday	Thursday	Friday	Saturday	Sunday	Totals
	Hours of attendance:	Hours of attendance:	Hours of attendance:	Hours of attendance:	Hours of attendance:	Hours of attendance:	Hours of attendance:	Number served:
	☐ Bkfst ☐ Snack ☐ Lunch ☐ Snack ☐ Dinner ☐ Snack	☐ Bkfst ☐ Snack ☐ Lunch ☐ Snack ☐ Dinner ☐ Snack	☐ Bkfst ☐ Snack ☐ Lunch ☐ Snack ☐ Dinner ☐ Snack	☐ Bkfst ☐ Snack ☐ Lunch ☐ Snack ☐ Dinner ☐ Snack	☐ Bkfst ☐ Snack ☐ Lunch ☐ Snack ☐ Dinner ☐ Snack	☐ Bkfst ☐ Snack ☐ Lunch ☐ Snack ☐ Dinner ☐ Snack	☐ Bkfst ☐ Snack ☐ Lunch ☐ Snack ☐ Dinner ☐ Snack	Breakfasts: _____ Lunches: _____ Dinners: _____ Snacks: _____
	Hours of attendance:	Hours of attendance:	Hours of attendance:	Hours of attendance:	Hours of attendance:	Hours of attendance:	Hours of attendance:	Number served:
	☐ Bkfst ☐ Snack ☐ Lunch ☐ Snack ☐ Dinner ☐ Snack	☐ Bkfst ☐ Snack ☐ Lunch ☐ Snack ☐ Dinner ☐ Snack	☐ Bkfst ☐ Snack ☐ Lunch ☐ Snack ☐ Dinner ☐ Snack	☐ Bkfst ☐ Snack ☐ Lunch ☐ Snack ☐ Dinner ☐ Snack	☐ Bkfst ☐ Snack ☐ Lunch ☐ Snack ☐ Dinner ☐ Snack	☐ Bkfst ☐ Snack ☐ Lunch ☐ Snack ☐ Dinner ☐ Snack	☐ Bkfst ☐ Snack ☐ Lunch ☐ Snack ☐ Dinner ☐ Snack	Breakfasts: _____ Lunches: _____ Dinners: _____ Snacks: _____
	Hours of attendance:	Hours of attendance:	Hours of attendance:	Hours of attendance:	Hours of attendance:	Hours of attendance:	Hours of attendance:	Number served:
	☐ Bkfst ☐ Snack ☐ Lunch ☐ Snack ☐ Dinner ☐ Snack	☐ Bkfst ☐ Snack ☐ Lunch ☐ Snack ☐ Dinner ☐ Snack	☐ Bkfst ☐ Snack ☐ Lunch ☐ Snack ☐ Dinner ☐ Snack	☐ Bkfst ☐ Snack ☐ Lunch ☐ Snack ☐ Dinner ☐ Snack	☐ Bkfst ☐ Snack ☐ Lunch ☐ Snack ☐ Dinner ☐ Snack	☐ Bkfst ☐ Snack ☐ Lunch ☐ Snack ☐ Dinner ☐ Snack	☐ Bkfst ☐ Snack ☐ Lunch ☐ Snack ☐ Dinner ☐ Snack	Breakfasts: _____ Lunches: _____ Dinners: _____ Snacks: _____
	Hours of attendance:	Hours of attendance:	Hours of attendance:	Hours of attendance:	Hours of attendance:	Hours of attendance:	Hours of attendance:	Number served:
	☐ Bkfst ☐ Snack ☐ Lunch ☐ Snack ☐ Dinner ☐ Snack	☐ Bkfst ☐ Snack ☐ Lunch ☐ Snack ☐ Dinner ☐ Snack	☐ Bkfst ☐ Snack ☐ Lunch ☐ Snack ☐ Dinner ☐ Snack	☐ Bkfst ☐ Snack ☐ Lunch ☐ Snack ☐ Dinner ☐ Snack	☐ Bkfst ☐ Snack ☐ Lunch ☐ Snack ☐ Dinner ☐ Snack	☐ Bkfst ☐ Snack ☐ Lunch ☐ Snack ☐ Dinner ☐ Snack	☐ Bkfst ☐ Snack ☐ Lunch ☐ Snack ☐ Dinner ☐ Snack	Breakfasts: _____ Lunches: _____ Dinners: _____ Snacks: _____

Publication 587 (2014)

Index

☀ To help us develop a more useful index, please let us know if you have ideas for index entries. See "Comments and Suggestions" in the "Introduction" for the ways you can reach us.